Teach Us to Pray

Overcoming Obstacles to Daily Prayer

Bradley Hanson

Augsburg ☐ Minneapolis

Library of Congress Cataloging-in-Publication Data

Hanson, Bradley.
    Teach us to pray : overcoming obstacles to daily prayer /
Bradley Hanson.
        p.   cm.
    ISBN 0-8066-2468-X
    1. Prayer—Christianity.   I. Title.
BV215.H35   1990
248.3'2—dc20   90-30769
                                                          CIP

The paper used in this publication meets the minimum requirements of American National Standard for Information Sciences—Permanence of Paper for Printed Library Materials, ANSI Z329.48-1984.   ∞™

Manufactured in the U.S.A.   AF 9-2468

94   93   92   91   90   2   3   4   5   6   7   8   9   10

To Marion,
my wife and best friend

Contents

Preface

"One day Jesus was praying in a certain place. When he finished, one of his disciples said to him, 'Lord, teach us to pray, just as John taught his disciples' " (Luke 11:1). It is always the Lord who teaches us to pray. Of course, the Lord uses Scripture and the lives, words, and experiences of others as pointers and guides, but ultimately the only real teacher of prayer is God. Prayer involves opening ourselves to God, opening our hearts to the Presence that loves us, and opening our eyes to see the Mystery that seeks our fulfillment in all circumstances. Only that loving, mysterious Presence is able to coax open our hearts and eyes. The events of life, the yearnings of the heart, and the words of others often are teaching aids used by God, but they have no effect unless God awakens us to greater spiritual openness.

There is no doubt that our need for learning to pray is very great. Prayer is far more than reciting specific prayers—it is communication with God, communication that is not merely passing information, but communion with God, which enables us to become more nearly our true selves. So prayer is not a technique that can be mastered. Learning to pray involves learning to trust

God in all situations. It involves learning from God's mercy to forgive ourselves and others and to draw ever more deeply upon God's resources for kindness and wisdom with family, friends, and coworkers. In the process we discover that God opens us to compassion and generosity with strangers. All these lessons—and more—take a lifetime to learn. The great reformer John Calvin said that in prayer we dig up the treasures God has for us in Christ. We never exhaust those treasures, for there are always more to find.

Learning to pray is a corporate process. As children we did our very first praying, if we prayed at all, by observing others and following their example. And now, even when we pray in solitude, we use the words and experiences of others. So when we encounter obstacles in prayer (and we all do), we may benefit from the insights of others who have dealt with similar problems. This book addresses a number of common obstacles to daily prayer and offers suggestions that have been helpful to me and to others.

My own ongoing education in prayer, including the writing of this book, is heavily indebted to others who have been my teachers in God's school of prayer. For more than a decade now the perceptions and questions of students in my Christian Spirituality class at Luther College have helped draw me ever more deeply into the living reality of prayer. Laity and clergy who have attended retreats with me have contributed by sharing from the wealth of their experiences. Their voices are heard in these pages. I am also grateful to the Franciscan sisters of Mount St. Francis and to the Trappist monks of New Melleray Abbey who have provided both me and my retreat groups with a hospitable, quiet space open for God. Judy Boese has made my life less stressful with her cheerful, highly competent assistance in computerizing the manuscript of this book. And throughout the production of the manuscript I have been supported by my wife, Marion, who, while managing the heavy dual responsibilities of job and motherhood, has also listened to my thoughts, forgiven my faults, and generally been God's gift to me. As these people have been helpful in my own growth in prayer, I hope this book will be beneficial to you and a useful instrument of the One who teaches us all to pray.

Introduction

One Saturday afternoon when I was twelve, my Dad called our family together in the living room—Mom, my brother, sister, and me. He said that he was not going to be living with us anymore, because Mom and he couldn't get along. Mom was crying.

This all came as a complete surprise to me. Our family had seemed happy and secure. We always did something special together for a summer vacation; usually we rented a cabin on a lake. Although we didn't talk much about God or religion at home, Mom and Dad took us to church every Sunday. And I never heard Mom and Dad argue or fight.

When Dad finished talking, he went to their bedroom and packed his things. In a while he came out with two suitcases and said to Mom that he'd have to pick up some other things later. He seemed cold, sort of businesslike. He loaded his car and said good-bye while Mom and we kids stood by helplessly. The final scene has been imprinted in my memory ever since—Mom standing in the driveway crying and looking after the receding car.

That night at bedtime I didn't say my prayers. I lay awake for a long time, but I didn't pray. It's been hard to pray ever since.

This man's difficulty in praying may not be the same as ours, but everyone who prays has some problems with prayer. To say that we never have prayer problems is like saying we never have family problems—neither is true unless we don't pray or don't have family. Prayer problems are not just narrowly religious problems comparable, say, to obstacles one might encounter in organizing a staff of church ushers or getting people to donate flowers for the altar. Such narrowly religious difficulties usually have little connection with what it means to be a Christian in daily life. A person could be a whiz at organizing ushers or flower givers yet not have the slightest clue as to what it means to be a Christian. Prayer problems are different, for they truly reflect the nature of one's relationship with God and the way in which that relationship affects the rest of life. The man who has found it hard to pray ever since his father left home is really angry with God, for he thinks God has let him down. His prayer life accurately mirrors this relationship with God; his resistance to prayer expresses his anger with God.

A common result of prayer problems is a gulf between a faith relationship with God and the daily experience of life. This is certainly true with the man who is angry with God. In a sense, he continues to believe in God, for he holds God responsible for the breakup of his childhood family. At the same time, however, he still pouts and refuses to talk much with God. As a result, he does not share the major and minor joys and sorrows, challenges and accomplishments of his life with God, and for the most part his life is deprived of the Lord's guidance and support. Instead of faith in God informing his daily relationships and responsibilities, a deep chasm exists between his life and his relationship with God. Not all prayer problems produce such a wide gulf, yet they do reflect some division between faith and life. Therefore, to face our prayer problems is to seek to build bridges and make connections so that through prayer God's light and power may flow more freely into all areas of life.

Even though we experience difficulties in praying, we tend to avoid facing them. We may hesitate because we are embarrassed to admit that we have such problems. After all, everyone should be able to pray—it seems so simple. For those who have leadership positions in the church, it is especially embarrassing to admit, for prayer is so basic to the Christian life. In part, we avoid facing our prayer problems because that might call for some major changes in our way of living. The man who is angry with God over his father's departure says that the only person he can rely on is himself. If he were to face his prayer problem, he would have to look squarely at his own sense of self-sufficiency and also deal with his anger. Such self-examination and change do not come easily, so we may put things off with a lame hope that somehow the problems will go away. We may also delay facing our difficulties because we do not know what to do about them or whom to consult for help. We may even have tried some new approaches to prayer in the past but found that they did not work out, and now we feel unsure of how to proceed, so we delay.

There are good reasons, though, to face our prayer problems. First, we are not peculiar; everyone who prays has prayer problems. To be sure, not all difficulties in prayer are equally serious, but over the course of a lifetime, everyone encounters some prayer problems. Second and most important, Christian prayer is always a response to the God who loves us and seeks our highest good. The Lord knows our reluctance to change and our mixed feelings about intimacy with God; we want to be closer, but we also want to control our own lives. Yet the Lord patiently seeks to draw us closer and to bring us more deeply into the reality of faith and prayer. Third, help is available. While this book does not claim to have all the answers, it casts new light on prayer problems and offers suggestions that have been helpful to others.

Although life includes peaks and valleys as well as plains, it is lived mostly on the plains; so prayer and its difficulties take place mostly on the plains. We will begin and stay on the plains for some time, for chapters 1 through 4 address some difficulties common to all forms of Christian prayer. We will descend into a valley in chapter 5 when we focus on the problems of praying in the context of suffering. Then in chapters 6 and 7 we will consider questions about petitionary prayer that can arise on just about any terrain. Throughout the following chapters we will seek to overcome the distances that often occur between faith and life by suggesting ways that prayer can bridge the gaps and better equip us for service in the world.

1

I Don't Pray Enough

THE MOST COMMON PRAYER PROBLEM IS THAT we do not devote enough attention to prayer. There is no way to specify what would be "enough," whether 10 minutes, 30 minutes, or an hour a day. Trappist monks and nuns normally spend several hours every day at prayer, yet sometimes they too feel they do not pray enough. So praying enough cannot be measured in minutes or hours. A serious feeling of not praying enough is probably a sign that we are not as much in touch with God as we should be.

My wife and I experience something like this in our relationship. Even though we are best friends, from time to time we fall out of tune. Sometimes one of us says or does something specific that causes a rift, but more often we simply get so preoccupied with our jobs that we gradually drift apart. When we become aware of the distance, we know that we have not been communicating enough and need to spend more quality time

together. In like manner, when we feel we are not praying enough, it may mean that we are out of touch with
God. This can happen because we have openly rebelled
against God and are no longer praying at all. It can come
about when we've been going through the motions of
a regular prayer time but haven't had our heart in it. Or
it can occur as a result of being so engrossed in other
matters that we don't pay much attention to the Lord
and so miss a sense of God's presence and direction in
our lives. However it comes about, a feeling of not praying enough means that, to some extent, we are out of
touch with God.

A Spiritual Struggle

Being out of touch with God is serious business, far more
serious than we usually realize. Paul's words in Ephesians 6:10-20 are like a highway sign or guidepost that
lets us know where we're at when we are out of touch
with God. Paul begins with this general advice: "Finally,
be strong in the Lord and in his mighty power" (v. 10).
His instruction is to find our strength outside of ourselves in God. Of course, it is very pious sounding to
say, "Trust in God. Rely upon the Lord." But this advice
in Ephesians is not just smooth-talking piety; it's based
on a real need.

"For our struggle is not against flesh and blood, but
against the rulers, against the authorities, against the
powers of this dark world and against the spiritual forces
of evil in the heavenly realms" (Eph. 6:12). Today we
do not see the world exactly as Paul and the other early
Christians did, nor is this required of us as Christians.
But it is clear that for them evil was so powerful that
humans by themselves cannot stand against it. It is common in our modern world to treat evil as though it were

manageable by human ingenuity and planning. Obviously some evils are subject to our control; we have made great progress against diseases such as polio and against social ills such as gross maltreatment of the mentally ill. Nonetheless, new diseases arise, nuclear weapons terrorize, drug addiction spreads, and death continues to reign over each one of us. It appears that the overall power of evil in the world is undiminished. What this means for us today is that part of our being out of touch with God is being unaware of the full power of evil. When we believe we can handle evil on our own, we do not pay much attention to God.

"Therefore put on the full armor of God, so that when the day of evil comes, you may be able to stand your ground, and after you have done everything, to stand" (Eph. 6:13). Because evil is so powerful, we are told to take God's own armor to defend ourselves against it.

> Stand firm then, with the belt of truth buckled around your waist, with the breastplate of righteousness in place, and with your feet fitted with the readiness that comes from the gospel of peace. In addition to all this, take up the shield of faith, with which you can extinguish all the flaming arrows of the evil one. Take the helmet of salvation and the sword of the Spirit, which is the word of God. (vv. 14-17)

Of course, twentieth-century warriors do not wear armor and wield swords, but the analogy holds true. Since this is a spiritual battle, the weapons must also be spiritual. Thus Paul then tells the Ephesians to "pray in the Spirit on all occasions with all kinds of prayers and requests" (v. 18). It appears that prayer is not a seventh weapon alongside the other six, but is a nonmilitary way to say what the military metaphor conveys: in this spiritual struggle use the resources of God. We are instructed to "pray . . . on all occasions." This is not just hands-folded, eyes-closed prayer; rather, all of life should be lived in the attitude of looking to God. Only then are we "strong in the Lord and in his mighty power."

Viewed in the light of Ephesians 6, the fact that we do not pray enough indicates more than poor scheduling on our part; it is also a sign of our reluctance to give full trust and loyalty to God. If we loved the Lord whole-heartedly, we would be in constant touch with God. But, the truth is that we have a heart that is divided between love of God and love of ourself, fame, or whatever. We are people with divided loyalties. Thus the foe is within us as well as outside of us. This reality lies behind all our prayer problems, so we must begin to face it right from the start.

The fact that we do not pray enough is not a minor breach of religious conduct like being sloppily dressed for church. All our prayer problems are far more than difficulties in technique, time management, or emotional adjustment. They are part of a spiritual struggle going on in our world and in our very own lives. Not praying enough means that we are in danger of losing the struggle. But *being aware* that we are not praying enough is a hopeful sign, for it shows that we have some sense of our danger and our need to pay attention to prayer.

Quiet Time

Paying attention to prayer begins with taking time for it. We are creatures of habit. Praying at bedtime and at mealtime are the most common prayer habits for us. If these customary prayer times are not enough for keeping in touch with God, then we have to take additional time, and it must become a fairly regular pattern or else it will die out.

However, taking time by itself is not sufficient. It must be the kind of time that favors giving attention to God. Two conditions that aid private prayer are solitude and silence.

A time of solitude is conducive to prayer, for it reduces the outside demands on our attention; other people are not beckoning us. Yet external solitude does not automatically produce prayer, for we can bring all sorts of mental companions into it—work plans, family worries, sexual fantasies, gossip. These companions have a way of occupying our minds so that we do not pay attention to the Lord even when we are alone. Thus the heart of solitude is not just being alone; it is an inner solitude in which we are alone with God and direct our full attention to the Lord. Ordinarily external solitude fosters inner solitude, but it is possible to be alone with the Lord while other people are nearby, say, in a city park or an airplane. The essential feature is a measure of confidence that others will not interrupt us.

Silence is also favorable to prayer, for voices and other sounds often distract us. But, again, mere external silence will not suffice, for we have a tendency to create a multitude of inner noises that distract our attention. What is needed is a stillness of the mind that allows us to focus for a while on God. It is also possible to have this inner silence at the same time as there are people talking, machines operating, or birds singing. The key is that the sounds do not disturb us. While it is hard to ignore someone speaking directly to us, a background of many voices in conversation may not bother us. Silence is so important for private prayer that it is common to refer to such a time as quiet time.

The chief purpose of having a time of solitude and silence is to put aside the ordinary round of concerns and to focus for a while on God. Of course, when we are engaged in our daily relationships and responsibilities, it is appropriate to give them our full energy and attention, for through them we live out our Christian ministry to others. God calls us to reflect Christ's love in the ways we relate to people and carry out our duties. But in order to reflect God's love and purpose, from time to time we have to turn our attention directly to the Source of that love and purpose. Doing this once a week on Sunday morning is not enough.

Jesus himself set an example. There is solid evidence that Jesus followed the traditional Jewish practice of praying three times a day—at sunrise, in the afternoon, and at bedtime. In addition to this daily practice and regular synagogue worship on the Sabbath, on occasion Jesus spent extended periods of solitude and silence in prayer. We remember first his hours in the Garden of Gethsemane when he left his disciples to pray, but Mark and Luke tell us of other occasions when Jesus went off to pray by himself. "Very early in the morning, while it was still dark, Jesus got up, left the house and went off to a solitary place, where he prayed" (Mark 1:35); and "After leaving them, he went up on a mountainside to pray" (Mark 6:46; see also Luke 5:16; 6:12; 9:18, 28). We are not meant to imitate Jesus in everything (such as his celibacy), but Jesus did teach his followers to pray. Therefore his example of setting aside times of solitude and silence for prayer should be taken seriously.

Taking Time

If we feel we aren't praying enough, we are certainly not peculiar, for our contemporary world puts all sorts of pressures on us that cause us to neglect prayer. We are discouraged from taking time for prayer by the pressure to always be on the go. Ours is a hyperactive culture. The individuals held up to us as models are usually superachievers. Chances are that even the elderly persons we most admire are very active people—no quiet reflection in the rocking chair for them. But if we're always busy, it's hard to find time for private prayer except in the few moments before we drop off to sleep at night.

Even when we have times that are not busy (and nearly all of us have some), it is easy to keep them from becoming occasions of solitude and silence. If we are alone at home or in a car, most of us are in the habit of turning on a television, stereo, or radio. Surely we all need some relaxation and entertainment, but often, without thinking of another option, we destroy the opportunities we have for a quiet time of prayer.

Since we live in a busy culture that seldom offers us ready-made occasions of solitude and silence, we may have to be creative in fitting a quiet time into our schedule. What works for one person may not work for another, but here is how some ordinary people take time for prayer.

An office worker takes 15 to 20 minutes of his lunch hour to go into a nearby church sanctuary. It's usually quiet there, and other people in the church don't bother him. It gives him a chance to collect his thoughts, and the symbols in the church help him focus on God. As a bonus he finds that frequently he comes out more relaxed and rested.

Jogging is an excellent form of exercise and tension release for one single mother and breadwinner; it's also her best time for prayer. She is an active person who finds it hard to sit still for very long, so jogging keeps her body busy yet frees her mind. As she works up a sweat, she can feel the tension slip away. She's alone and she's generally not distracted by the people and things she passes. As she relaxes, she turns to the Lord with the concerns of the day.

Her late afternoon walk is the main prayer time for a college student. Except at bedtime it's very hard to pray in her dorm room. Even when she has the room to herself, she never knows when one of her two room-mates will pop in. Her walk gives her some time alone. When the weather is nice, she takes her pocket New Testament along and stops along the way to read some Scripture. If the weather is bad, she tries to read a bit of Scripture before she sets out. She does not get out for a walk and prayer every day, and that's okay.

John gets up about 20 minutes early so that he can have quiet time for prayer before his child's stereo begins to boom out. Several times he had tried to establish a prayer time later in the day, but it always fizzled out; other things got in the way, and he could never really form a habit. Finally he decided to get up earlier in the morning. It was not easy at first. He didn't feel like getting out of bed any earlier, but after a week or two his body adjusted and he got into the habit of going to bed a bit earlier. He still catches up on his rest by sleeping in on weekends, but now on workdays he looks forward to that quiet time.

If the traffic is not too heavy during her 40-minute drive to work, Jennifer leaves her car radio off and de-votes some of these minutes alone to meditation and prayer. Usually there is a stretch that doesn't require edge-of-the-seat alertness. This gives her time to bring her concerns before the Lord and to ponder God's will for her day.

Taking time for prayer may not be easy at first. Finding the minutes is not the greatest obstacle—they are there somewhere. The main barriers are within us, in our priorities and habits. The first big step is to make a commitment to a regular prayer time. Is being in close touch with God a high priority? If so, we will find the time. The next step is forming a new habit of prayer. This is often hard, because our bodies and personal clocks do not readjust without complaint; but once the new habit is formed, we generally look forward to our quiet times. Some trial and error may be necessary before finding a quiet time that will actually work. And even after finding one, we should be prepared to give it up for another. We may not keep the same quiet time indefinitely. As circumstances change, so do times for prayer.

Having a regular quiet time for prayer would be a dreary affair if God were a hard-to-reach executive and regular prayer were just a way to get God's attention. Fortunately, God is accessible. Jesus encourages us to come to God in prayer: "Ask and it will be given to you; seek and you will find; knock and the door will be opened to you" (Matt. 7:7). God wants us to be in close touch, and prayer is the basic means of communication.

When we have a regular quiet time for prayer, we frequently find ourselves making momentary prayers at other times during the day. Becoming more aware of the Lord during that usual time commonly makes us more aware of God at other points in the day as well, so we find ourselves in brief conversations thanking God for this thing or asking God to help that person. In ways that we can neither anticipate nor understand, God brings us into closer touch through prayer.

2

My Prayers Are Repetitious

HEAVENLY FATHER, BLESS MOM AND DAD, AND bless Jerry's mom. I thank you, Lord, for Jerry. Help him to be more patient with the kids. Watch over the kids and keep them safe; help them to know that we love them. Bless Uncle John, Aunt Louise, Aunt Bernice, Mr. and Mrs. Murphy, and Mrs. Andrews. Help me at the office tomorrow, and forgive me for any wrong I've done this day. In Jesus' name, amen.

The words of this bedtime prayer are not identical with our own, but chances are that our bedtime prayers, like this prayer, remain much the same day after day, year after year. We tend to get into a pattern in our bedtime prayers, and while individual items in the prayer change somewhat, the basic pattern doesn't change. Even individual items often stay unaltered. The woman whose prayer is reprinted above probably has been asking God to "bless Uncle John" for forty years. When one of my sons was in primary school, out of sheer habit he continued to pray for the recovery of a neighbor long after being informed of the man's death.

Repetition in prayer is not necessarily a bad thing. Jesus taught his disciples the Lord's Prayer, and Christians have prayed it repeatedly with benefit for centuries. Table prayers are generally very much the same from meal to meal, and they would not necessarily be better if different words were used each time. Even in everyday speech, the sincerity of a "thank-you" does not require new words but a real attitude of gratitude. In like fashion the genuineness of a prayer depends much more on the attitude of the person praying than on the originality of the words. In short, repetitious prayers are faulty only if one does them mechanically, mouthing the words but not praying with the heart. Even this is not a major problem if it is occasional and short lived; from time to time faith may lag for a bit but soon revive. But when most or all of our praying is mechanical repetition, then we have a serious prayer problem.

Long-lived, mechanical repetition produces two deadly offspring. The first is that we end up having little real communication with God; even though we take time to talk to God, what we say has no real meaning. The second is a dichotomy between faith and life. Changes take place in our lives and in the lives of others we know, but our prayers remain about the same. If our prayers suffer from mechanical repetition, then we have a problem that we need to face.

Spiritual Indecision

Sometimes when we call a doctor's office and ask to make an appointment, a receptionist says, "Will you hold, please?" Then as elevator music fills the silence, we are left waiting. Being on hold is an in-between status. No one can or will speak with us right now; yet we are kept waiting. A receptionist could break off communication entirely by declaring that they don't want our business and then saying good-bye. When we are put on hold, it means that we must either wait until someone is ready to speak with us or hang up.

When our praying is limited to mechanical repetition day after day, we are putting God on hold. If we wanted to break off relations with God, we would stop praying altogether. And if we were ready to truly communicate with the Lord, we would not merely go through the motions of praying. Sustained, mechanical repetition in prayer is a manifestation of spiritual indecision, in which faith and unbelief contend and neither is able to win a clear victory.

Since long-term, unthinking repetition in prayer is fundamentally a spiritual disorder, it is necessary first of all to look within ourselves for the cause. What has been happening in our relationship with God? We can discern three points along a spectrum of indecision. First, there is spiritual inertia. Inertia, the tendency of something to resist motion, action, or change, can overtake a friendship or marriage. At one time the two people were quite close, but somehow gradually the relationship became stagnant and they drifted apart. Many of the outward forms of the relationship persist—they do and say many of the same old things, but the life has gone out of them. What was appropriate and meaningful some time ago is now hollow. Inertia can also plague our relationship with God; what was a close bond has now become distant. Prayers that once were fresh become dry and stale. Automatic prayers say, in effect, "God, I don't know what to say to you now." This is the middle ground on the spectrum of indecision; one's relationship with God might either revive or die.

A second point on the spectrum of indecision is doubt. One may have a deep longing to converse with God but is racked with doubts, other commitments, or possibly even bitterness. One is not ready to give one's heart fully. In such a state of doubt, to pray one's usual prayers is an act of nursing faith so that it may grow stronger. Putting God on hold with a repetitious prayer in this case is an unspoken plea, "Please, Lord, wait for me." This is a hopeful state.

Mechanical prayer might also flow from a third point on the spectrum of indecision: prayer as a memento that one is not quite ready to throw away. From time to time one takes out the memento and remembers what used to be but puts it away again. The object doesn't fit into one's present life. Putting God on hold with a mechanical prayer in this situation is like saying, "God, I'm too busy with other things now, but there's a slight chance I'll have time for you later." Such a prayer mostly projects unbelief. It is perilous indeed to be in this state, for it is close to rejecting God completely.

Putting God on hold through sustained, repetitious prayer delays full communication with God. Central to this is a refusal to deal with the underlying spiritual disorder. Thankfully, a fuller understanding of prayer can help us break out of the dull pattern of mechanical repetition, even as it works to heal the underlying spiritual condition and bring new life to our relationship with God.

Prayer As Dialog

We usually think of prayer as talking *to* God. We talk and God listens. Indeed, worship services foster this idea, since during those parts of the service designated as prayer, the congregation speaks directly to God. However, a fuller understanding sees the heart of prayer as dialog or conversation with God, where both parties speak and listen. The dimension of prayer in which we listen to God is called meditation.

The basic way to get out of the rut of mechanical repetition is to strengthen the listening or meditation side of prayer, for when we listen well to God, we become more aware of God's presence and activity, and our faith is strengthened. The New Testament is clear that faith comes by hearing the Word of God. When we meditate on the Word of God as it comes to us in Scripture or through other means, faith can grow.

If we are putting God on hold, our relationships with God will only worsen—unless we have new exposure to the Word of God in some form. When we put God on hold we rely on the religious ideas we invent for ourselves or pick up from the popular thinking of our day. We create our own version of God's will, a version that usually supports and justifies our present way of life. Then true faith is starved. But listening to the Word of God nourishes faith and gives it new strength.

When we listen to God, the speaking side of prayer naturally flourishes. When we have a fresh appreciation of God's goodness and our trust in the Lord is revived, thoughts and words come to us readily. It's like what may happen when we meet a person who was a close friend a long time ago. That close friendship was built on understanding and trust, but we don't trust someone who has become a near stranger to us. However, if time is spent getting to know that person again, trust is revived and intimacy returns. Listening and being attentive can bring a rebirth of trust. Similarly, when we listen to God, there is an opportunity for trust to be renewed. Then we have no difficulty speaking to God.

Unfortunately, the word *meditation* may evoke images of strange postures and exotic practices; we may identify meditation with Eastern religious practices. As a matter of fact, though, nearly all of us at times engage in religious meditation, even though we may not call it that. Whenever we reflect on God's relationship with us and the world, we are participating in religious meditation. We can do this without quite realizing what is going on, because the meditation occurs spontaneously. It can take place as we ponder a decision at work, gaze upon an age-lined face in a crowd, see a photograph of a starving child, or witness a beautiful sunset. We did not set out to meditate; it just happened.

If we want to strengthen the listening dimension of prayer, we must also practice some forms of planned meditation. Chances are that we already do some planned meditation without giving it this name, for attending worship services and church classes implies some desire to hear God speak to us. But if we are already doing these and feel a need to deepen our dialog with God, then we should take up some forms of individual, planned meditation.

Ways of Listening

There are more ways of listening to God than can be treated here, but we can look at four kinds of private listening. We often do not know what will work for us until we try it.

1. Reading. The members of a farm family—Joe, Lois, their children, and two grandparents—illustrate several ways to listen to God through reading. Joe reads a book of the Bible from start to finish by taking a paragraph or two or even a whole chapter per day. This *continuous reading* doesn't involve formal study of the text, but it does require some degree of attention to the words. Joe reads the text or portions of it a second time and then allows a few minutes of "soak time" by considering what

29

the Lord would have him hear from these words. It's seldom exciting, but Joe has found that over the months and years it has had a considerable impact. Every year he's able to read several whole books of the Bible and reflect on their message. He finds that stories, images, and ideas that he's read come back to him at other times, and he feels that his understanding of God has been enriched. One great advantage of continuous reading is that it can be done in as little as 8 to 10 minutes, so he can usually work it into his day even during the busiest periods.

Lois and her elderly mother listen to Scripture by hearing it read on *cassette tape*. Some of the time Lois spends driving to her job in town she uses for listening to a reading of a book of the Bible. Since her mother's eyesight is poor now, they share the same Scripture cassettes. Both are accustomed to replaying portions and stopping the tape to ponder what they have heard.

Grandpa employs an *imaginative reading of Scripture*. He takes a story in the Bible and tries to create the scene in his imagination. If it's the story of Joseph being seized by his jealous brothers and sold into slavery, Grandpa imagines the voices of Joseph's angry brothers as they strip off his sleeved, long robe and cast him into a pit. He hears the sound of their sandals on the stones around the pit and the thud of Joseph's body landing on the bottom. He sees the fear and surprise in Joseph's eyes. Grandpa either imagines himself as one of the characters in a biblical scene or as an extra person alongside them. When he has created the scene in his mind, Grandpa finds that he is usually more open to what God has to say through the story. Often he rereads the passage of Scripture and replays the scene in his mind with new details. He can easily spend half an hour on a single story.

Matthew, the oldest son in the family, intersperses his reading of the Bible with reading good *devotional literature.* He reads a variety of things—prayer books, biographies, or studies on Christian life. Like the rest of the family, he allows time to reflect on what he's read. He wants time to pay attention to what God might have to say through his reading as well as time to respond to the Lord.

2. *Writing.* Some people love to write, and many more find that writing helps them clarify and focus their thoughts. It is not uncommon to discover that what jumbles and whirls about in our minds takes on shape and meaning as we put it into writing. There is a creative dimension to writing as well, for putting things into print quite often helps us see connections that we might otherwise miss. Writing also draws things out of us that we find difficult to say openly. These assets of writing are recognized in the contemporary Marriage Encounter movement, which seeks to enhance communication between marriage partners by each partner writing the other a letter. These strengths and others make writing a marvelous means for listening to God.

I know a man who has been writing down his biblical meditations for about 30 years. He has no intention of publishing them and does not ordinarily show them to anyone. They are meant for God and himself. This man reads a biblical text from a list of daily Bible readings, but rather than just turn the passage over in his mind, he uses a pencil to express his thoughts. Sometimes he draws a diagram. The writing and drawing help him to see connections in the biblical text and focus his attention. He dates his entries so that he can later look back to see how his thinking has developed. So what he really does is keep a *biblical journal,* for the starting point of each entry is a scriptural text rather than his own daily experience.

A *personal spiritual journal* begins with one's own experience. Most commonly a daily entry begins with a short summary of the outward events of one's life and then moves into some reflections on those events, how one thinks and feels about them. One's own dreams can also be very fruitful material for a journal. Keeping a log of one's experiences, however, does not constitute meditation. What makes the journal a form of spiritual listening is to place the day's experiences before God and to ask what the Lord wants to say in and through these events, responses, or dreams. Morton Kelsey, who has kept a spiritual journal for 30 years, says, "I find I start a day awry when I do not bring the summary of my life and inner thoughts and dreams before the one who wishes to relate to me. As I pause and listen, something other than my ordinary typical habitual attitudes speaks within me" (*Adventure Inward*, Augsburg, 1980). A spiritual journal is not for everyone, but many find it immensely valuable. About a year after I suggested journaling to a Christian Spirituality class, two of the students went out of their way to tell me how fruitful it had become for them.

3. *Following a daily liturgy.* Some Christians build their quiet time around a liturgical form that they can say alone. This practice is most common among those from a church with a tradition of daily liturgical forms such as Morning and Evening Prayer in the Anglican and Lutheran traditions. This approach might seem to increase repetition rather than reduce it, yet there is more in this practice than might appear at first glance. For one thing, these liturgies are composed mostly of psalms and other Scripture readings that vary with the day. Hence someone who uses Morning Prayer for a year, for example, is exposed several times to the psalms and once to many other parts of the Bible. If the person observes a time of silence after each reading, there is ample time for listening to God. Furthermore, the prayers addressed to God in these liturgies lift us beyond the limited circle of concerns in our own prayers to larger concerns. Thus, while some say that a daily liturgy is

too formal and lacks variety, others discover that it provides a stable framework for listening to the Word of God.

4. *Taking a retreat.* If two intimate friends fall into the rut of saying the same routine things to one another and seldom get to anything deeper, one method of breaking out of the rut is to go away by themselves for a few days and renew their friendship. Although it's difficult to manage this when there are children to consider, my wife and I have done this from time to time. In effect, we take a retreat from our jobs, children, and community in order to give more attention to each other.

A retreat can also be a good way to break out of the pattern of repetitious prayers that don't communicate. For this to be accomplished, though, the retreat must be the kind that allows a person to focus on God rather than being kept busy by a full schedule of events. In many churches, what is called a retreat is a workshop or conference. These events reflect the hyperactive nature of our culture by filling almost the entire time with a busy schedule of group sessions. This is like a married couple going off to visit relatives for a few days; the couple is together but is so seldom alone that each has even less time for the other than when at home. A true retreat should provide ample time for solitude and silence so that we may listen to God. Tuning in to God on a retreat requires tuning out the sounds and static that normally fill our ears.

This is the logic behind the outward and inward shape of a retreat. What is done outwardly varies somewhat depending on the type of retreat. Some retreats have group sessions that provide food for thought and guidance for the quiet periods. On another kind of retreat a person spends an hour each day with a spiritual director who can hear concerns about one's journey of faith and give specific suggestions for individual reflection. Or a person can spend a day or more without any given structure, devoting the whole period to what is commonly done in the quiet periods of any retreat—get some extra sleep, read Scripture and other books, walk or jog, sit quietly in a sanctuary, or perhaps chat a bit with others. These external actions are the peel of a retreat, but the fruit is inward and invisible—dialog with God. Most of what we do inwardly on a retreat is wait for God to speak to us. We listen for God, and when God speaks to us we find ourselves replying in fresh ways.

Obviously retreats cannot be frequent experiences, and they are no substitute for daily conversation with God, but as occasional complements to daily prayer, retreats can revitalize our relationships with God and enrich the dialog of prayer. I myself have made at least one retreat per year for over a decade, and every time it has been the occasion of a renewed sense of God's presence and purpose.

Listening to God through a regular practice of individual meditation is an effective remedy not only for long-term mechanical repetition in prayer, but it is also a central part of the remedy for any prayer problem. Meditation is highly beneficial for persons in any spiritual state. Christian faith draws life from the Word of God. In this respect Christian faith is like a child's love. A child learns to love by receiving love from others; the child's love is a response to love. Imagine a 10-year-old girl who has been consistently mistreated by the people around her. She will be unable to show love to others. It's not a matter of the abused girl making up her mind to love others, she simply does not have the resources to love all by herself. On her own she is truly unable to love another person. If she ever comes to love another human being, it will be in response to receiving love. In similar fashion, Christian faith is a response to God's love as expressed in some form of God's Word. All by ourselves we cannot simply "decide" to have faith, for we are unable in a vacuum to give our trust and loyalty to God without first hearing of God's love and mercy. Thus it is absolutely vital for us to listen to the Word as it comes to us in Scripture, preaching, the sacraments, hymns, books, or the informal witness of other Christians. Individual planned meditation is an immensely valuable form of listening to God.

One of the marvels of the Christian message is that it tells us that God searches us out and seeks our response. God is the shepherd who goes after the one lost sheep and the woman who searches her house for the lost coin (Luke 15:3-10). God seeks us with a Word of compassion, strength, and acceptance and invites us to listen and respond.

3

My Mind
Wanders

I SAY THREE PRAYERS PRACTICALLY EVERY NIGHT BEFORE going to sleep. They include Martin Luther's Evening Prayer, the Lord's Prayer, and my own prayer, which varies depending upon my worries, appreciation, and general mood.

My problem with saying evening prayers is that I often end up daydreaming during them. For example, on any given night, Martin Luther's Evening Prayer might be: "I thank Thee my heavenly Father, through Jesus Christ, Thy dearest Son, our Lord, that Thou hast graciously kept me this day. (I wonder what's for breakfast tomorrow. I hope it's Egg McMuffin.) And I pray Thee that Thou would graciously keep me this night. (I hope I can finish my math before class.) For into Thy hands I commend myself, my body and soul, and all things. (I wonder if Jeff will call tomorrow. He'd better.) Let Thy holy angel be with me that the wicked foe may have no power over me. Amen."

Occasionally, when I'm worried about something, like a potential breakup with my boyfriend, I'll daydream but make sure to emphasize certain lines. For instance: "Our Father, who art in heaven, hallowed be Thy name.

Thy kingdom come (I hope he's not still mad at me. I hope this is for the best.) Thy will be done (Maybe we'll work things out), on earth as it is in heaven."

All too often, though, I find myself just stopping and starting all over again. It's not that I don't want to pray, it's that I can't concentrate and make my prayers meaningful. I think that if I had a stronger religious faith, then I would be able to speak with God and give him my full attention.

Everyone who prays struggles with the problem of a wandering mind just as this young woman does, yet we tend to be sheepish about admitting it. We value sincerity and authenticity in religious expression, so we hate to admit that we often say our prayers with our minds on something else. We prefer to interpret a wandering mind as a temporary lapse rather than a deep-seated flaw, so we minimize it and expect to overcome it sometime in the future. The truth is, however, that on this side of heaven we will always have to contend with our wayward attention. A wandering mind in prayer is a sign of a wandering heart.

A Wandering Heart

If we have to drive a long distance, we find that after awhile it's hard to keep our mind on the road. A coffee break may help revive our attentiveness, but no matter what we do, at some point our bodies require sleep. There are times of great danger or excitement in which our attention span is extended beyond the normal, but these are exceptions. There are real physical limits to how long we can be awake and fairly alert.

Hardly any of us, though, can claim that our lack of attention in prayer stems from sheer physical exhaustion. Although we may be physically tired when we come to pray, that is usually because we have left prayer till the last moments of our day, not because we've been praying for hours. A wandering mind in prayer says far more about our priorities than about our physical condition.

What we are attentive to reflects our interests and concerns. Since I very much enjoy playing tennis, I will watch a good tennis match on television for a couple hours. To someone who has no interest in tennis, the same match would be utterly boring. Again, if one of my children is involved in a public event at school, I pay close attention to it because I care about my children. If God were indisputably the greatest strength and joy of my life, then I would be fully attentive in prayer. A wandering mind in prayer is mainly the product of a heart whose loyalty to God is unsteady.

Gethsemane Drowsiness

Jesus' disciples also suffered from wandering minds and hearts.

> Then Jesus went with his disciples to a place called Gethsemane, and he said to them, "Sit here while I go over there and pray." He took Peter and the two sons of Zebedee along with him, and he began to be sorrowful and troubled. Then he said to them, "My soul is over-whelmed with sorrow to the point of death. Stay here and keep watch with me."
> Going a little farther, he fell with his face to the ground and prayed, "My Father, if it is possible, may this cup be taken from me. Yet not as I will, but as you will."
> Then he returned to his disciples and found them sleeping. "Could you men not keep watch with me for one hour?" he asked Peter. "Watch and pray so that you will not fall into temptation. The spirit is willing, but the body is weak." (Matt. 26:36-41)

This was crunch time for Jesus and the disciples. Jesus knew that his arrest and death would come soon. He also sensed that within these events he faced the ultimate spiritual test of his life. It appeared to be God's will that he die, but he did not accept death easily. Would he remain faithful to God?

If the disciples had been alert to what was going on, very likely they would have prayed fervently. They probably knew that they risked being seized and killed, but they seemed unaware that they were also being confronted with a great spiritual test: would they be faithful to God by being faithful to Jesus? Indeed, they were confident that they would stand up to the severest trial. Shortly before they went to Gethsemane, Jesus said they would all fall away. "Peter declared, 'Even if I have to die with you, I will never disown you.' And all the disciples said the same" (Matt. 26:35). Heedless of their spiritual peril, the disciples slept. Peter, James, and John especially should have been awake to the situation, for Jesus had charged them to "watch" with him (v. 38) and again later, "Watch and pray so that you will not fall into temptation" (v. 41). Yet they too slept. It was more than physical fatigue; spiritual drowsiness closed their eyes to their spiritual danger.

In their heedlessness the disciples failed to pray and thus were unprepared for the critical moment. When the test came, "all the disciples deserted him and fled" (Matt. 26:56). In contrast, the watchful Jesus devoted himself to prayer and so was ready to face his betrayal and death.

Jesus' command to Peter, James, and John applies to us all: "Watch and pray so that you will not fall into temptation." What is translated as *temptation* is often rendered as *trial* or *test*. However it is translated, the truth is that we cannot prevent a temptation, trial, or test from happening any more than the disciples could

prevent Jesus' arrest. What we can do, however, is prepare to meet the temptation or test when it comes. Prayer
is the way we prepare. When we pray, we are putting
on the armor of God so that we may be able to stand
when the test comes. As Paul says in Ephesians 6:18,
"Pray in the Spirit on all occasions with all kinds of
prayers and requests. With this in mind, be alert and
always keep on praying for all the saints."

Spiritual Watchfulness

Spiritual watchfulness, the foundation for prayer, pre-
pares us for the tests of life by discerning what the tests
are. Spiritual watchfulness is not the same as the vigilance that enables us to survive in the world. As children
we were taught vigilance when parents and teachers
told us to look out for strangers and cars; as adults we
are taught it by law enforcement agencies that warn us
to be on guard against fraud and violence. And no one
teaches us to be wide awake when our life is threatened
by disease or assault; the desire to survive is instinctive.
While vigilance for survival is very important, it is not
the watchfulness of which Jesus speaks. In fact, because
the disciples obeyed that survival instinct, they forsook
Jesus and fled. As Jesus shows in his parable of the
dishonest steward who after he was fired made friends
for himself by reducing the bills of his master's creditors,
the children of darkness are more clever survivors than
the children of light (Luke 16:1-13).

The watchfulness of which Jesus speaks is alertness
to the spiritual dangers, opportunities, and resources
present in a certain situation. While they slept in Gethsemane, the disciples were oblivious to the risk that, in
their weakness of faith, they would abandon Jesus. They
did not even seek God's aid. To be watchful today means

to be on the lookout each day for the spiritual hazards and opportunities in our specific situations. A story may help illustrate the nature of spiritual watchfulness.

When Robert first heard that his company would announce a promotion the following week, his heart began to beat faster. Hope and fear were mixed together. He wanted the promotion desperately, and he had good reasons to think he was likely to get it. His work had been of a high quality and he got along well with most people; he even felt that the boss liked him. But Alvarez and Sullivan were also in the running. Robert didn't really like either of them, but he had to admit they were good at their jobs. So he worried. What if he didn't get the promotion? It would be humiliating to lose. Losing had always been hard for him. But the long-term consequences were even more serious. Robert might never rise beyond his present level. The thought terrified him. A big part of his life would be over, finished. He would have to go on working to pay the bills, but he would no longer be advancing. The race would be ended for him, and all he could do then would be to run in place. Maybe he could start fresh somewhere else—another company or even his own business. But at his age and with all his financial obligations, could he do it? The uncertainties scared him.

It so happened that at church that Sunday the sermon was based on Mark 10:35-45, the passage that tells about James and John asking Jesus to let them sit in the places of honor at his right and left when he came into his glory. Robert had heard the story before, but this time it spoke to him in a special way, provoking serious reflection. He had made winning and getting ahead one of the central goals of his life. Was the promotion really that important? Even if he got it, he knew he wouldn't be satisfied; he'd push on to win something else. Trying to be a winner was a never-ending rat race. It also pained him to think how his competitiveness had harmed relationships over the years. Because he had to come out ahead, he always felt like he had been in a contest with anyone who challenged his preeminence. But now the words of Jesus pointed out a very different way of living: "Whoever wants to become great among you must be your servant" (Mark 10:43). Could he do that? Could he give up his competitiveness? Not on his own surely, but with God there must be a way. He would pray about it.

At first Robert feared only failing to get the promotion. Very likely he had no difficulty keeping his mind on his prayer when he asked God for success. Survival vigilance produces its own kind of attentiveness in prayer, for we are fully awake when our vital interests are at stake. I recall an ordinarily nonpraying high school pal saying that he prayed with great fervency his girlfriend would not be pregnant. But his attention was narrow in scope and short-lived. He prayed only about the possible pregnancy, and as soon as that crisis passed, he stopped praying.

Spiritual watchfulness makes for greater attentiveness in prayer, for it broadens the scope of our interests and concerns. It awakens us to hitherto unperceived threats much as Robert was aroused to see how competitiveness was twisting his life. Watchful prayer can also open our eyes to see the needs of the hungry, thirsty, and naked of the world; and with enough growth we may even be alert enough to recognize Christ present in them (Matt. 25:31-46). There are ample opportunities and threats that call us to pray with full attention. In our family, neighborhood, workplace, club, church, nation, and world we learn of people who have needs and for whom we might pray. Spiritual watchfulness enables us to see those needs and be attentive to them in our prayers.

The difficulty is, of course, that watchfulness does not come easily. It is sobering to remember that at Gethsemane the disciples did not even realize they were being tested until it was over and they had failed. This is the way it is with us much of the time. Robert saw the evils of competitiveness only after they had harmed his personal relationships. Peter failed the Lord many times before he emerged as a courageous apostle. Our weakness is not hidden from Jesus. He said, "The Spirit is willing, but the body is weak" (Matt. 26:41). To the extent that we are led by God's Spirit, we have the watchful sight of faith; but we are also frail flesh with very limited vision. Our divided heart gives rise to partial sight and wavering attention.

Nonetheless, God does not give up on us, just as Christ did not give up on the disciples. Even though Peter and the other disciples fell away as Jesus expected, he forgave them and sent them out again to be watchful. As Paul says, "Be alert and always keep on praying" (Eph. 6:18). Like sentries we are called to be on guard for anything and to stay at it. Our moral and religious training helps us recognize the obvious friends and foes, but much is unexpected or camouflaged by the customary. It takes a sharp eye and perseverance.

What this means in practice is that the first line of defense against a wandering mind in prayer is taking time to discover or recall the needs, opportunities, and threats in our specific situation. To plunge immediately into our standard prayer forms without taking even a few moments to search the landscape is bound to result in daydreaming. Again, paying attention often to the Word of God in Scripture and as it comes to us through the wisdom of others is critical, for it sharpens our eyes and ears for picking up the signs. Robert would not have perceived the evils of relentless competitiveness if he had paid attention only to the mass media and popular opinion, for our culture promotes competitiveness as a virtue. Another light was required to expose the truth. Thus, as a practical prelude to prayer, spiritual watchfulness involves two things. One is frequent attention to the Word of God to sharpen our senses. The other is taking time before prayer—perhaps only a couple minutes—to search the landscape for signs of opportunity, blessing, or danger.

Other Tactics

Another tactic that works well as a prelude to prayer is suggested by the seventeenth-century Spanish mystic, Teresa of Avila. She suggests that we remind ourselves to whom we are speaking when we pray. For instance, if we were given the chance to meet with the president of the United States or the queen of England, we would have no difficulty in giving our full attention to the meeting, especially if it were a private audience. If we remind ourselves that in meditation and prayer we meet with the Lord of the universe, then we are likely to be alert. To be realistic, however, we have to expect that this tactic will lose its effectiveness if it is used too often. Somewhat as White House staff members in frequent contact with the president soon take his presence for granted, so we tend to take the privilege of prayer for granted. Yet, used occasionally, this tactic can be effective.

Even though certain preludes to prayer can increase our attentiveness, we will still find our minds drifting during prayer. There are two broad strategies for dealing with these distracting thoughts. One strategy is to crowd out the diversion and hold our attention on God. One way to do this is to fight off the distraction with a repeated word or sentence. This use of a repetitive prayer has a long history. For example, the Jesus Prayer ("Lord Jesus Christ, have mercy on me") has its origins in the fifth century and has been especially cultivated in Eastern Orthodox churches. An anonymous fourteenth-century English author wrote *The Cloud of Unknowing*, which recommends repeated use of a single word such as *God* in prayer. A prayer formula may seem strange to many people, especially those who recall Jesus' warning against heaping up empty phrases in prayer. Yet Jesus seems to have in mind the insincere prayers of persons who "think they will be heard because of their many words" (Matt. 6:7). But a prayer formula can be an authentic form of Christian prayer when used in faith.

One advantage of a prayer formula is that it can help direct a person's attention to God. The mind needs to focus on some object, and the prayer formula acts as an object friendly to prayer. Usually one does not ponder the meaning of the formula itself, for one would soon be bored and would search for other thoughts. Rather, the prayer formula acts like a lens; one doesn't look *at* the lens but *through* it. So the main function of the prayer formula is that it directs one's attention toward the Lord and holds it there.

As soon as one becomes aware of having been distracted, one returns to the formula. Sometimes a mental tussle ensues, but one can use the formula as a weapon to fight off the distraction. Indeed, some Christians use a prayer formula to fight against the most serious distraction—a temptation—so for them it becomes a way of heeding Jesus' teaching, "Watch and pray so that you will not fall into temptation."

The second broad strategy for handling distracting thoughts in prayer is to bring some of them into our prayers. When I am bothered by distractions, I sift through them. Mostly they are about trivial matters—a play in a ball game, what I'm planning for the evening; these I try to push aside. But sometimes the other thought is about a weighty matter, and then I bring it into my prayer. For example, if I am concerned about a troubled student, that student becomes part of my prayer. I may pray for the student with specific requests. Or if I am using a prayer formula, I will insert the student's name into the formula, so that, as I look through the lens of the formula, I am holding that person up before God.

This second strategy connects faith and our day-to-day responsibilities and relationships. When we relax a bit, as we usually do when we pray, the issues of life come bubbling up from within—anxieties and hopes, hurts and thanks. If we keep all these thoughts out of our prayers, we build a wall between faith and life. But if we select the truly significant thoughts that bubble up and incorporate them into our prayers, faith has the chance to influence life. When we pray for others, we are more likely to relate to them in constructive ways; so prayer strengthens us for service to others. And when we let our worries and hurts enter into our prayers, then God uses prayer to minister to us.

Finally, in addition to spiritual watchfulness and specific prayer tactics, we need patience and perseverance in contending against a wandering mind. No matter what we do, praying is often like driving at night through a snow storm. Our efforts to clear away the distracting thoughts are about as effective as our windshield wipers in removing the snow. If the snow is not too heavy, we can manage to see the road and move ahead. Sometimes there is even a break in the flurries, and we can see clearly for a while before the swirl returns. Once in a while the snow gets so thick that we are stalled completely. Certainly if we become impatient and recklessly speed up, the road disappears altogether in a white cloud. We must learn to be patient, for the snowflakes will continue to come at us. We must "be alert and always keep on praying" (Eph. 6:18). In any case, we are not alone. Everyone else on the road has to cope with the storm as well, and even though we may not be aware of it, the Lord is with us.

4

I Pray
Yet God
Seems Distant

IN THE FILM <u>FIDDLER ON THE ROOF</u>, TEVYE, A RUSSIAN –Jewish farmer who delivers milk in the village, complains mildly to God when the horse pulling his milk cart goes lame.

Dear God, was that necessary? Did you have to make him lame just before the Sabbath? That wasn't nice. It's enough you pick on me—bless me with five daughters, a life of poverty. That's all right. But what have you got against my horse? Really, sometimes I think when things are too quiet up there, you say to yourself, "Let's see, what kind of mischief can I play on my friend Tevye?"

He also complains to God about his poverty. Would it spoil some vast eternal plan if he were a wealthy man? When each of his three oldest daughters breaks with tradition in choosing a husband, he debates his own stance on the matter in dialog with God. When persecution strikes Tevye's Jewish community, he takes his troubles to God and wonders, "Who do you take your troubles to?" With words or just a heavenward look, he is in nearly constant dialog with God. When he prays, Tevye usually looks upward to the sky, but God is not far away above the clouds; God is close at hand, an intimate companion who shares Tevye's life.

At times we may experience prayer like Tevye does. God is close, and praying is an intimate conversation with a dear friend. At such times prayer flows freely, our faith seems strong, we feel our lives supported by God and filled with meaning. When we have a solid sense of God's presence with us, prayer is easy. Most of the time, however, we lack a lively sense of God's presence. Usually God seems farther away, sometimes even very distant. Then prayer is more difficult; it may have the humdrum character of the routine, or God may seem so far away that prayer becomes nearly impossible. Our awareness of God's presence affects prayer so much because communion with God is a basic dimension of prayer. Besides listening and speaking, prayer is also communion with God.

Communion with God

A boy growing up with loving parents who affirm him and seek his well-being is powerfully affected by them. The atmosphere of their love is always there, whether or not the boy recognizes it. Mom and Dad love him when he is a newborn baby and not yet familiar with them. They care for him as a young boy, even when they discipline him. They continue to surround him with love when he becomes a teenager, though he often ignores them and sometimes clashes with them. At times he is keenly aware of and appreciates his parents' love and opens his heart to them. Whether he realizes it or not, he is strongly influenced by the loving atmosphere his parents create.

When we live in any social atmosphere for a considerable time, we adapt to it and are changed by it, whether we know it or not. For instance, we learn to speak our native language, but we absorb more than we realize. As soon as we speak, someone with a good ear can quickly identify what part of the country we come from and perhaps even our ethnic or economic backgrounds. We participate in our social atmosphere in ways that go far beyond what we consciously recognize or choose.

This is true also in the family. When we get to know a friend's family, it is common to see that similar mannerisms, phrases, attitudes, and habits are often shared by family members. This was brought home to my wife and me once when we attended a dinner party at which we met the parents of an acquaintance I'll call Virginia. At the dinner table Virginia's father dominated the conversation. If we strayed into an area foreign to him, he'd soon steer the conversation back into his territory with another long story. Throughout dinner Virginia's mother always deferred to her husband, hardly saying a word. After dinner we broke up into little conversational groups of two or three, and my wife ended up spending the rest of the evening with Virginia's mother, who, like her husband, began to talk incessantly. On our way home in the car my wife commented, "Now I know where Virginia gets her nonstop talking." Virginia had patterned her behavior after her parents' without ever deciding to do so and without being aware of it. Children participate unconsciously as well as deliberately in the ways of a family.

This is also true of each Christian's communion with God. According to the apostle Paul, life in Christ is similar to living in an atmosphere of parental love. Paul thought of Christ as being truly present to the believer in the reality of his crucified and risen life. So when Paul speaks of "fellowship" (Greek *koinonia*), what he has primarily in mind is fellowship with Christ as the believer shares in Christ's life. As an atmosphere of parental love fosters the well-being of a child, so the presence of Christ is the atmosphere in which the Christian life exists and thrives. By living in this atmosphere, we participate in Christ's life and share his character by dying and living with him (Rom. 6:8). We participate in Christ deliberately, but we also share in Christ's character without being aware of it. Whether we receive Christ's love knowingly or unawares, that love brings us into communion with God.

We have communion with God because Christ is able to be personally present with us and for us. Christ's presence *with* us is not just a physical presence (for a rock or a stick of wood can be physically present), but Christ is personally present. Two people can be together in an elevator and yet not be personally present to each other. If they communicate through speech or gestures, then they become personally present to one another.

This "communicated" presence comes in different intensities. We speak of some persons as having "presence," for they make their presence known and felt by others; they are forceful persons who make an impact on other people. On the other hand, a person can be present in different intensities at various times. For example, a woman who is normally forceful in public might be so self-absorbed at a meeting that she lacks personal presence ("She wasn't really with us today"); she was there but did not make her presence felt. The same person can have a private and public presence, speaking with her best friend in a way quite different, for example, than the way she would speak to a large group. One's presence is conveyed in varying intensities through words, gestures, and actions. Of course, how one's presence is perceived also depends on the receptivity of the other person. Many preachers and teachers know this, for the very same talk can be perceived by one person as dull and lifeless yet by another as powerful and dynamic.

Christ is personally present with us when we hear the Lord speaking to us and when we feel we are getting through to God in our prayers. However, this requires that we have a rather clear awareness of God's presence, and this is precisely what is often lacking. Often we have little sense of God's presence with us.

Yet God continues to be personally present *for* us as well as *with* us. A social worker shows a special interest in a boy in trouble with the law by going to bat for him with the police and the judge. The boy doesn't know all that the social worker has done for him and may not appreciate what he does know about; nonetheless, the social worker has been personally present *for* that boy. An elderly woman whose husband has Alzheimer's disease keeps an eye on him as he sits on the porch in the afternoon. She makes sure that he doesn't leave a cigarette in the wrong place or wander away somewhere. Even though he doesn't realize how much attention she gives him, she is personally present for him.

To be present for another is the foundation for constructive and good communion. The delinquent boy already has contact with destructive elements in his environment, but if he ever becomes friends with the social worker and picks up good attitudes and habits from him or her, it will be chiefly because the social worker has been present for the boy. It is likewise God's presence for us that is the ground of our communion with the Lord. "At just the right time, when we were still powerless, Christ died for the ungodly. Very rarely will anyone die for a righteous man, though for a good man someone might possibly dare to die. But God demonstrates his love for us in this: While we were still sinners, Christ died for us" (Rom. 5:6-8). Without our deserving it and prior to our awareness or consent, God was acting on our behalf, seeking our welfare. This divine presence for us is the basis of all our communion with God.

Since prayer usually involves some sort of conscious listening or speaking to God, it is strongly affected by our awareness of God's presence with us. Prayer varies greatly as our awareness of the Lord's presence fluctuates. We are at a high point when we, like Tevye, sense the Lord close at hand; prayer comes easily. This is why Christians in charismatic or Pentecostal groups who have had a recent, vivid experience of God's presence testify to such a strong desire to pray. When our sense of the Lord's presence diminishes, prayer comes with difficulty. When God seems distant, both the listening and speaking dimensions of prayer feel like they are taking place with a remote partner or no partner at all. We try to listen to God, but we don't hear much; we speak, but God seems not to hear us. But most prayer takes place between the extremes, and God is neither near nor far.

Since our own awareness of God's presence with us is not a reliable gauge of the full scope of our communion with God, we should learn not to rely upon it too much. What is steadfast is God's presence *for* us. Whether we feel God is near, distant, or in between, God is always seeking our well-being. The key is not to identify God's presence with a certain kind of religious experience, but to trust that God is present for us throughout the fluctuations in our awareness of God's presence *with* us. Whether God seems near or far, we can still listen for God and speak to God.

When God Is Near

Strange as it might seem to someone outside of the church, experiences of special intimacy with God are neither well understood nor universally valued among Christians. Many Christians from traditional churches who became involved in the charismatic movement found that when they told their pastor or fellow church members about their experience of a vivid presence of God, they met with a cool reception. In many church circles, mountaintop religious experiences are viewed with skepticism and suspicion. At the same time, in other church groups mountaintop experiences are told and retold with fervor and are held up as the key to the Christian life. What we need is a balanced outlook that appreciates peak moments when they come without making them the center around which communion with God and prayer are supposed to revolve.

While news stories about fanatical religious groups have taught us not to believe every claim to close encounters with God, we should know that God wants to be present with us. God does not want to be distant. In fact, God has often promised to be present. We can take Haggai's words to Israel as God's promise to us as well, " 'Be strong, all you people of the land,' declares the LORD, 'and work. For I am with you,' declares the LORD Almighty. 'This is what I covenanted with you when you came out of Egypt. And my Spirit remains among you. Do not fear' " (Hag. 2:4-5). The many instances in Scripture of God being intensely present to individuals and communities make it clear that God wants an intimate relationship with us.

Furthermore, many people have had at least one experience of special nearness to God at some point in their lives. It probably was not as vivid and startling as Moses' meeting with God at the burning bush (Exod. 3) or Paul's confrontation with the risen Christ on the road to Damascus (Acts 9:1-9). It may well be that hardly anyone else knows about it, for like other deeply personal matters, it is a closely guarded secret. Nonetheless, experiences of an unusual closeness of God are common enough not to be dismissed as merely the products of sick minds.

It is not at all surprising that experiences of special intimacy with God frequently happen under the conditions we identified earlier: solitude and silence. In these situations we tend to be more receptive to God's presence. Moses was doing the solitary work of a shepherd, Paul was with travel companions but on a long journey likely to produce extended periods of quiet. In my own experience, I am most likely to have a strong sense of God's presence when I make a personal retreat; usually after a day or so of slowing down and waiting, I become aware of God close at hand, and we enter into sustained dialog. In the weeks and months following the retreat, if life is not too hectic, this sense of God's presence continues; it is most apparent when I take a walk alone, but it is also the background for frequent brief conversations with God in the midst of the day's activities. Only very seldom do I have a vivid awareness of God's presence; generally it is more of a quiet assurance that God is close at hand. In either case, prayer is spontaneous.

The same linkage between a strong sense of God's presence and ease of prayer is reflected in this testimony of a man involved in the charismatic movement.

> Mary Lou and I are twenty-seven years old. It took Jesus that long to break our stony hearts and give us hearts of flesh. But he has! Since this experience we have begun to grow in his love, in his peace and joy. His presence and his power have transformed our lives. He has given us faith.
>
> He has given us a gift of praise and prayer. Both of us had tried for a long time to lead prayerful lives without much success. But God has begun to lead us in prayer with an ease and depth and consolation we never knew before. (Kevin and Dorothy Ranaghan, *Catholic Pentecostals*, Paulist Press, 1969)

Whatever the character of a person's experiences of unusual intimacy with God, the chief issue is how we regard them and their significance for prayer. Some people look back on such experiences as the high points of their lives. Like former athletes who dwell on bygone days of glory and never accept normal life, they live for moments of religious glory and avoid the mundane routine of prayer. Some people, on the other hand, are fiercely proud of the fact that they have never been powerfully aware of God's closeness. Like veteran football linemen who never made the headlines, they revel in their toughness; no flashy stuff for them. Wary of any peak religious experiences and suspicious of those who have them, such people see the crucified Jesus as one who kept his head down and slogged it out in the mud. For them prayer is nothing but plodding.

It is far better to see experiences of special nearness to God as similar to those moments of intimacy and great happiness that occur from time to time in a good marriage. To make such moments the foundation of a marriage relationship would be foolish indeed, for they come and go quickly without our bidding. Yet it would be equally foolish to despise such moments and be closed to anything but the pedestrian ways of everyday married life. When seen as fleeting samples of the happiness that is possible in complete mutual love, the high points of a marriage revitalize and strengthen the commitment of the partners to one another. So, too, a moment when we sense God is very near is like a taste of heaven, which rekindles on earth our love for God and breathes new life into our communication with the Lord. Certainly prayer will not always be as spontaneous and satisfying as when we sense God is near, but those moments of profound fellowship with God help us see the great value of prayer even when God seems farther away.

When Prayer Is Routine

Most of the time we have neither a strong sense of God's presence nor a painful awareness of divine absence; usually God seems to be in the vicinity but not intensely present. Prayer takes on a more humdrum quality. In many ways, our everyday prayers are like day-to-day communication with a good friend. We don't have deep heart-to-heart talks every day with that friend, for we are not often intensely present to one another. Most of the time we talk about common things such as daily events, mutual friends, and ordinary responsibilities. Nothing dramatic takes place in these conversations, yet they keep us in touch with one another, and when a serious concern does arise, we naturally go to that friend.

Most of our listening and speaking to God has a similar routine quality. If we attend church, usually nothing makes a strong impact on us. If we read the Bible, only occasionally do the words speak powerfully to us. Listening to God through worship, Scripture, or devotional books is generally routine. And speaking to God in prayer is just as unexciting as our meditation; prayers at church as well as our private prayers are usually rather humdrum. Because nothing much seems to happen in these routine activities, we might overlook their long-range value.

Think for a moment of what often happens between close high school or college friends after they graduate. Two old school friends end up living at some distance from one another. When they get together once in a while, some of the old rapport is still there. Yet over time their lives have grown further and further apart as each has experienced new places, activities, and people unknown to the other friend. Now when they meet they are unlikely to speak about deeply personal things; they will turn to someone else who knows them and their situation better. They have grown out of touch.

Routine prayer—prayer in the broad sense of all our listening and speaking to God—keeps us in touch with God. At times we might be so troubled by its drab, habitual character that we consider dropping it altogether; but that would be a mistake. Without routine listening and speaking to God individually and with other Christians, God would become a stranger to us; then if we tried to speak with the Lord, we would find ourselves stuck in the superficial conversations we usually have with strangers. We would fall out of touch.

In addition to speaking to God, the central ways to keep in touch with the Lord are listening to God's Word and receiving the Lord's Supper. We become aware of other persons through the signs that make their presence known—their bodily presence, words, and gestures; without these signs we would not perceive their presence. God's presence for us and with us is communicated especially through Scripture, Baptism, and the Lord's Supper, for God has promised to be present with these signs. God is present everywhere and at all times, but very few of us are always alert to that general presence. We need to come to those points where the Lord has promised to focus the divine presence: Scripture and the sacraments. Here we can count on God's presence, and if we are receptive, we will be aware of that presence.

We learn of God's thoughts as God's Word comes to us through Scripture and the interpretation of Scripture, so paying attention to Scripture and to people who have a sound understanding of God's message is vital for staying in touch with God. As we noted in chapter 2, listening to God is the foundation for speaking to God; both keep us in touch.

The Lord's Supper has unique encouragement for us in our routine communication with God. In the Lord's Supper, Christ is present with us and for us in several ways: in the words from the Last Supper, in the gathered community of believers, in the minister representing

Christ, and centrally in the bread and wine. Christ promises to be present here whether or not we sense it. It is appropriate that we often refer to the Lord's Supper as Holy Communion, for it is the perfect example of our communion with God. Some days the Lord's Supper gives us a vivid awareness of Christ's presence; other days we go through it without sensing anything happening. Either way, when we participate in the Lord's Supper in faith, we have communion with Christ. The benefits of Holy Communion do not rest primarily on our changing consciousness of God but on God's firm promise to be with us and for us in the Lord's Supper.

When God Seems Remote

Another time we must trust that God is present for us is when God seems remote. One woman shared her difficulties in relating to God after her husband's sudden death in a car accident.

For about two weeks after my husband was killed I was in shock; it didn't really hit me what had happened. Making the arrangements for the funeral was like planning for any other big gathering. I had to find places for people to stay and that sort of thing. Only several days after the funeral did it sink in that I would never see him again.

Then I went into a long period of disorientation. I felt that I'd undergone an amputation, I'd lost part of myself. I'd always done so much with him—we made most decisions together, we went most places together. Suddenly he wasn't there, and I felt confused, disoriented. It's like I'd been heading in one direction for a long time and then I was spun around and around in a circle, and I didn't know what heading to take. I only knew it was impossible to go in the old direction.

During the early part of this disorientation period, especially when I'd go to bed at night, my heart would ache so much it would hurt. In fact, my whole body ached, but it was concentrated in my heart. I thought I might have to see a doctor about it, but I never did, and gradually the aching went away. Outwardly I must have appeared normal, because people would say to me, "Oh, Irene, you're doing so well." And I suppose outwardly I was. I was teaching, and I continued to go to school everyday. But I didn't really know what I was doing in the classroom; I couldn't plan. In my state of confusion, my students carried me through. But inwardly I had this ache.

I prayed every day, but I didn't know what to say or what to ask for. During this whole time, I felt very much supported by the church—members of my own congregation and also other Christians too. I felt supported by their prayers. But myself I didn't know what to say to God.

Irene's story expresses what many of us go through when we undergo a major trauma: God seems rather far off and our prayers sputter or cease altogether. Some traumas strike suddenly—death of a loved one, the announcement that a spouse wants to separate, a serious accident or disease, loss of a job, or a move to a new place. Other things creep up on us gradually, such as the accumulated stress of giving long-term physical care to an invalid in the family, the never-ceasing demands of mothering and job, or the helpless feeling of being trapped in a bad situation we cannot change. Whatever the circumstances, the trauma of them puts us off balance. Like Irene, outwardly we might appear in control of things, but inwardly we don't quite understand what has hit us. We may continue to go through the motions of prayer just as we go through other motions of normal life, but our hearts and minds are somewhere else. It is not at all surprising that at such times we would feel

God has moved some distance off and that prayer falters, for prayer reflects what is going on in our lives. When we are off balance in daily life, we will likely be off balance in prayer as well. Prayer falters mainly because in this state we are rather unreceptive to God's presence.

Trauma is not the only cause for a person feeling God is remote; it can also come about by a falling away resulting from faithlessness. But someone turning away from God does not seek God's presence. It is different for the person with some measure of faith who desires to pray and would like to sense the strength and comfort of God's presence, yet feels that God is remote. Such a person is pushed into this position by the force of trauma. Trauma can knock us off balance. The question is, How can we regain our balance?

The support of other people helps steady us. God has created people to support each other, and this support comes in a myriad of ways: a neighbor brings a casserole; a friend offers to take the kids for a weekend; a family member lends a sympathetic ear; an agency sends a person once a week to care for a home-bound person, giving the primary care-giver a break. Irene noted that her students helped carry her through. We cannot solve all our problems alone, nor can we create the support we need, but we can receive it. We need others.

Just as we may receive support from others for our physical and emotional needs, so there is also aid for problems of religious faith and prayer. Irene speaks of this. Norman does, too:

> When my first wife died, I couldn't pray for a long time, but it wasn't a loss of faith—I'm sure of that. God seemed absent, yet I didn't lose faith. I couldn't pray. I didn't have the words; I didn't know what to say or what to ask for.
>
> The worship services of my church and the prayers of the people carried me through. I felt sustained, lifted

up, buoyed up by their worship and prayers. I couldn't pray. They prayed for me.

In the context of Christian community, a person is upheld by the faith and prayers of others and, through them, by Christ. The Christian community provides unique support since it is, as Paul says, the body of Christ (1 Cor. 12:12-30). This suggests that, in a special way, Christ is present in the church, acting in and through believers to steady someone who has been struck by trauma.

That God should act this way is thoroughly consistent with the Incarnation, for Jesus' heavenly origin was not obvious. He must have spoken with a Galilean accent and dressed like other people from his culture. Yet Christians believe there was an unsurpassed presence of God in this outwardly unspectacular human being. Similarly today God is present to us in and through people who meet our needs, even though they may be ordinary people with imperfections and perhaps even annoying habits. God ministers to us in a special way when we experience trauma and find it difficult to pray; besides serving us through the kindness and abilities of others, God also supports us through the prayers of fellow Christians. While we may feel as though God is coolly observing us from a considerable distance, God is present with us and for us, hidden in the people who care for us and pray for us.

Another way to be steadied by God when we are knocked off balance and find ourselves unable to pray in our usual way is to pray by simply letting ourselves "be" before God. This is like what we do if we come to spend some time with a person who is grieving after the recent death of a loved one. We don't know what to say, because words are inadequate for the situation. So we say very little. What counts is being there, and words are useful only to the extent they help show that we feel for the grieving person. Similarly, when we ourselves are hurting and at a loss for words in prayer, we can just let ourselves "be" before God.

One way to do this is to say nothing in prayer except to acknowledge our confusion: "Well, God, here I am (again). I don't know what to say. I don't know what to think about all this. I don't even feel like praying. But here I am anyway. Do with me what you will." Then just sit, lie, kneel, or walk under God's eye. It's good to do this in the presence of some symbol, such as a cross. These symbols remind us of God's love in Christ, for they are tangible signs of a divine presence that we, at the moment, do not feel. Instead of or in addition to tangible symbols, it is possible to repeat a word or sentence such as the Jesus Prayer, "Lord Jesus Christ, have mercy on me," for the words help direct our attention to God. Whether or not we repeat such words, in essence we are lifting up our confusion before God. We don't need to know what to say to God or what to ask for. We can let our confusion itself be our prayer by holding it up before God.

5

What Sort of God Would Let That Happen?

ONCE WHEN I WAS AT A CONFERENCE IN CHIcago, I took a break one evening and I went to a concert with an old friend. After the concert, since my friend and I were staying in different places, I headed off alone toward a downtown hotel. I got onto a side street in a seedy area with very few people around. Suddenly, a half block ahead of me, two big men came out of a bar. They stood in the middle of the sidewalk talking, looked around, and then fixed their gaze on me. Should I turn around or cross the street? Indecision let my feet carry me closer. Finally I decided to press ahead, my body tense. When I came within a few feet, one of them said, "Sir, do you know what time it is?" Still walking briskly, I told him the time. They both smiled, thanked me politely, and turned away to discuss their plans.

My belief that the two men were dangerous affected my brief relationship with them. But the same principle is at work in our relationships with other people and with God. If we believe that a physician is competent, we will trust his or her medical advice. If we're convinced that an auto mechanic is dishonest, we'll take our car elsewhere for repairs. Our concept of God also has a powerful impact on our relationship with God; our mental picture of God can foster or inhibit prayer.

Of course, our ideas of others are not purely rational, for they are influenced by deep, often unrecognized, feelings. My fear of the two men on the street was based largely on my feelings about the seedy area of the city; seeing two men step out of a bar in a posh neighborhood would not have caused me alarm. Similarly, the way we think of God is partly rooted in deep feelings. If God is associated with positive feelings, we are comfortable approaching God in prayer. But if God is linked with fear, hurt, or rejection, dialog with God is much more difficult.

Fortunately, our views of others are not fixed forever, for new experience can dramatically alter our outlook. The polite words and behavior of the two men dispelled my fear. A serious blunder by a physician undermines confidence. Events and experiences likewise modify our understanding of God. Thus understanding, feelings, and experience interact in our relationship with God, and they powerfully influence prayer. This fact was brought home to me by Martha, who had taken a theology class from me some years before. We had not kept in touch, although I had heard that now she was married and had several children. One day she called and asked to see me.

Martha's Story

"It's been a little more than two years since my son Mikey died—it was two years a week ago last Friday. I wasn't at home when it happened, but I can still see it in my mind. Mikey was playing ball between our house and the Zimmermans' with some other boys from the neighborhood like they often did. The Zimmerman boy hit a long one that rolled all the way into the street, and Mikey ran after it. If we told him once, we told him a thousand times to always stop and look both ways before going into the street. But he was excited because it was the last inning of the game and the score was close. A pickup truck with one of those covers on the back was parked there, and he ran in front of it. There was a car coming up the street, and the driver didn't see Mikey until it was too late.

"For months afterward the scene played over and over in my mind. I could hear the screech of brakes and feel the car as it hit his little body. I wanted to run to him and hold him. I wondered, Oh, God, why couldn't it have been me? Only eight years old. Why couldn't it have been me?

"When it all sank in, I was so mad that sometimes I felt I'd explode. I'd say awful things, use words that I'd never used before. Never when the kids were around, only when I was alone or with Frank. I wanted to know why God hadn't done something. It wouldn't have taken much. Only a second or two difference in time and Mikey would still be alive. I wondered what sort of God would let that happen. I'd always thought of God as someone who took care of us, watched out for us. Of course, I knew lots of bad things happened in the world, but they had always happened to other people, never to me. I'd been taught that God loves us, and to me that meant God would protect those who had faith in him. I hadn't really thought it all out; it was more like something I took for granted.

"Then I really got mad at my brother, Roger, who works with the postal service. Ever since he's been involved with a new church, he's talked about God having a plan for our lives. When Roger first started work at the postal service, his supervisor was nice to him and helped him out a lot. To hear Roger tell it, God had placed that man there just to help Roger. Then when that supervisor was transferred, that too belonged to God's plan; God wanted to teach Roger how to cope with an unhappy, irritable supervisor. That's the way it was with Roger—he believed God was arranging all the details of his life, even down to getting a parking spot on a crowded street. Well, Roger came to Frank and me and told us that Mikey's accident was a part of God's plan for our lives.

"I thought about that, and the more I thought, the madder I got. If God had planned Mikey's death, then I didn't want anything to do with him. Any God who'd take the life of an eight-year-old boy in order to teach his parents something is not a God that I could pray to. Where's the love in that? I can't see it. It's been hard for me to talk with Roger ever since.

"For a while there I thought of God as an observer. I still believed that God had created the world, but I thought after that God just watched. I felt that there is no master plan to things, no big purpose. Whatever purpose there is, we make for ourselves—you know, like loving your family. Even then I thought a lot of it is just plain luck; we have to do the best we can with the cards dealt to us. The man who lives on the corner of our block has a bad heart; just a walk around the block leaves him breathless. It runs in his family—heart trouble—his dad died young with a bad heart, and so did his brother. Right next door to him lives Elsie McGivern; she's 84 and spry as can be. She mows her own lawn and brings us cookies from time to time. Her mother and father lived to a ripe old age, too. We have to play the cards we get. Elsie was lucky; she got a better hand than the guy with heart trouble.

"It's strange, though, that all the time I believed that God is just an observer, I continued to pray almost every night before I went to sleep—just like I'd done since I was a child. I didn't say much in the prayers; mostly I repeated what I'd said for years. Then it came to me that it doesn't make sense to pray to a God who just watches, doesn't care what happens to us, and doesn't do anything. I was tempted to quit praying, but I didn't. Maybe I didn't really believe all that stuff about God being merely an observer, maybe that whole idea was another way of expressing my anger.

"Things started to come together for me this year during Lent. My anger had cooled down quite a bit by that time, and I was trying to make some sense out of things. Now I knew better what I did *not* believe about God: I didn't believe in a God who steps in to keep us safe from all harm, I didn't believe in a God who planned Mikey's death, and I didn't believe in a God who doesn't care what happens to us. But what could I believe about God? During Holy Week I was thinking about the suffering and death of Jesus when it occurred to me that God didn't intervene to save Jesus from the cross. In the Garden of Gethsemane Jesus prayed that this cup would pass from him, but God didn't step in to stop it. Now there is a lot to this that I don't understand, but one thing stood out crystal clear—God let his own Son die. I can feel the car as it crashes into Mikey's body, think what it must have been like for God when those nails cut into Jesus' body. God knows what suffering is; God feels it as one who also suffers. God could have prevented it all, both for Jesus and for himself, but he didn't. That means we're not meant to be sheltered from all harm. Believing in God doesn't shield us from the pain and sorrow of life, but God isn't shielded from that pain and sorrow either. I know that somehow God feels my suffering and suffers with me. Believing this didn't make me miss Mikey any less, but I felt as though God were cradling me in his arms and feeling the loss as much as I. I'd never felt the presence of God so strongly before. I didn't want to leave when church was over. I just sat there, tears running down my face. Frank seemed to understand; he took the kids out to the car and waited for me. Since then it's been easier to pray. It was as though a dam had cracked, and all my pent-up thoughts and feelings flowed out. I feel God's presence once again, and prayer is often like being with a dear friend."

After Martha told me her story, it was plain that God had already begun the healing process with her, and in many ways she simply wanted to share her thoughts and feelings with me. Yet she also had a number of doubts in her heart and questions in her mind that needed working through, so we agreed to meet once a week to talk through them.

God on the Inside

The next Monday morning in chapel at Luther College it was announced that the infant son of a staff couple had suddenly died the previous evening. The reason was still unknown, but the harsh reality was all too clear—young David was dead. As I got up to leave, I noticed a colleague standing silently alone by the rear wall. He seemed very pensive and was making no move to leave. When I reached the lobby I saw a staff couple embrace—she with tears in her eyes, he with a sad expression of comfort. They were not close friends of David's parents, and I wondered at their reaction until I remembered that some years ago their first child had died. Then I also remembered that over 20 years before the pensive man in chapel had lost a young child in a car accident. Late that same day I walked back to my office with yet another colleague who said that he felt especially weary because his body had been aching all

day for David's parents. The news had certainly sad-
dened me, but it hadn't had such a physical impact on
me. Then he reminded me that years earlier he and his
wife had lost a child at birth.

It was clear that those who had lost a child knew
what David's parents were going through. We who had
not gone through such an experience were able to listen
and imagine what it is like, but those who themselves
had lost a child understood with immediacy and viv-
idness. For them the news opened old wounds, mem-
ories, and emotions. Forgotten physical responses were
reawakened and surged anew through them. The past
came alive in the present. They who had lost a child
knew the experience from the inside; the rest of us knew
it only from the outside.

Our capacity to share in another's experience of losing a child tells us something about God. Although we
are prone to think that God is outside of our lives, the
truth is that God is inside our experience. Even when
we feel God is interested in us and knows what is going
on with us, we tend to think of God doing these things
from the outside. In reality, though, God knows us and
our suffering from the inside. Indeed, God knows us
from the inside far better than any human can.

To some extent we human beings are always outside
of each other's experience. After more than 25 years with
my wife, I know her much better than when we were
first married and am more adept at detecting when she
is troubled; nonetheless, I still have to wait for her to
tell me exactly what is troubling her and what her particular feelings are. Even those people who themselves
had lost a child did not know exactly what David's parents were feeling, for those others had had a *similar*
experience but not precisely Karen and John's experience
of losing David. Indeed they ran the risk of thinking
Karen and John's experience was identical with their
own. While all of them share the reality of losing a child

that gives them a special sensitivity to this tragedy, God is the only one who knows our particular suffering fully from the inside.

God did not spare Jesus from suffering. "He was despised and rejected by men, a man of sorrows, and familiar with suffering" (Isa. 53:3). God's unique presence in Jesus shows us something immensely important about God's character: God does not stand off at a distance but gets deeply involved in suffering.

Furthermore, God suffers even when we ourselves are not aware of any discomfort. In this respect God is like a good and wise mother who sees her daughter go through a rocky adolescence. Not only is she sad when the daughter is unhappy, but the mother may even grieve when the daughter feels she is doing just fine. The grief is over failings to which the daughter is simply blind—unkindness, selfishness, missed opportunities to do good. Likewise, in addition to suffering *with* us, God also suffers *over* us.

I am often amazed by the unending patience of God. Attention is usually given to the suffering and death of Jesus as the focus of God's suffering *for* people when God took our place, a substitutionary suffering. Just as wonderful is God's patience in suffering *over* us. Parents usually get a taste of this when their children go through adolescence. Yet most adolescents become reasonably responsible adults, so the parents can relax and stop suffering over their children. But in relation to God, all of us remain adolescents; God can never relax and feel we can stand on our own. God continues to suffer over us, enduring our failures and lackluster performances with amazing patience.

This understanding of God has great significance for prayer. For one thing, since God suffers with us and knows our suffering from the inside, we are encouraged to pray and to pray honestly. God already knows when our anger is hot or our despair is strong, so we would do well to follow the example of biblical writers who pour forth these feelings to God in laments. In Jeremiah 15:18 the prophet cries aloud: "Why is my pain unending and my wound grievous and incurable? Will you be to me like a deceptive brook, like a spring that fails?" Likewise, the psalmist cries to God: "Awake, O Lord! Why do you sleep? Rouse yourself! Do not reject us forever" (Ps. 44:23). Imagine the nerve of telling God to wake up and notice what's going on. Jesus himself used a biblical lament when he cried out from the cross, "My God, my God, why have you forsaken me?" (Ps. 22:1). The Scriptures encourage us to voice even our anger and frustration to God.

Since God knows our suffering from the inside, it is beneficial to use prayer forms that help us bring our hurts to God. The typical bedtime prayer list does not give God much of an opening to work further healing in our lives. But one could, for example, meditate on the story of Jesus healing the paralytic who was lowered down to him through a roof.

Instructions for such a meditation could be as follows:

- For the first couple times allow at least an hour for this meditation.
- Be alone in a quiet place and get relaxed.
- Recall a time in your life when you felt close to God. Recall that experience in detail and let yourself feel again God's love and supportive presence.
- Read the story of the paralytic (Mark 2:1-12). Imagine yourself as the paralytic being brought into the presence of Jesus. Look at the kindness in Jesus' face.
- Offer your "paralysis" to him. Let the feelings come up out of the depths of your soul—even hurt, sorrow, and anger. Lay them before Jesus and ask for his healing.
- Healing will seldom be instantaneous, so do this often enough to allow God to make progress.

Why Does God Allow Suffering?

If a tragedy happens, employees appreciate having a boss who is kind and sympathetic. But what if the boss could have prevented the tragedy in the first place? Most likely we would be angry with the boss and would find it hard to accept any sympathy. Similar thoughts about God can intrude on prayer and meditation or even stop our prayers altogether.

Although we can never make all the pieces fit together, three main ideas can aid us in understanding why God allows suffering. These insights can help us continue in prayer even when suffering comes.

First, much suffering is a negative side effect of our freedom, which God allows us to exercise even when it costs us or others dearly. While some suffering is caused by things in nature, much is caused by human beings. The suffering caused by some misuse of human freedom ranges all the way from a simple error in judgment to well-planned evil, and the fruits include accidental deaths, violent crimes, social oppression, and war.

We ought not to blame God for suffering produced by human error or ill will. We who prize so highly the opportunities opened up by our freedom ought not to expect God to rescue us whenever someone might misuse it. In the story at the beginning of the chapter, Martha was right to reject her brother's picture of God as one who directs all the aspects of our lives; it seems to make freedom an illusion. Worse yet, a God who plans all the events in the world would also be responsible for Mikey's death and all the other evils of the world. As Martha asked, Where is the love in that?

Just as a loving parent gives a growing child greater freedom in order to develop the child's capacities, God gives us room to make our own choices. God allows us to use our limited freedom, not because God doesn't care, but because God loves us. God rejoices in our wise choices and grieves over the foolish ones.

But even so, we often wonder why it is that people often do not deserve the humanly caused suffering that strikes them. Sometimes suffering comes as the just consequence of the evil behavior of oneself or one's group; a criminal merits some kind of punishment, a ruling class that exploited the poor deserves defeat. In such cases we can see a moral order and righteous judgment at work. Yet frequently the suffering seems unfair. Should an eight-year-old pay with his life because he chased a ball out into the street? In addition, people frequently endure suffering brought about by someone else's error or malice; Martha also suffers from her son's mistake. A Salvadoran child is crippled by a land mine planted in a war conducted by others. Why is so much humanly caused suffering distributed unjustly? While we may find no satisfying answer to this question, it remains true that humanly caused suffering is a negative side effect of our God-given freedom.

A second idea that helps us remain faithful in prayer is that suffering caused by nature is usually not sent by God.

I know a woman whose first child died at birth. This woman, a Christian, rejected the suggestion that this was God's will, and she found comfort in the idea that each day there was a certain percentage of babies who would die, and hers was just one of the unfortunates in that percentage. As Martha pointed out, nature in some ways operates somewhat like a card game; there is a strong element of chance in the way talents and liabilities, strengths and weaknesses are parceled out by heredity. But there is also a powerful element of consistency or law in nature. Just as a card game is not governed by chance alone, for there are rules that give each game its own character, so nature is a combination of chance and law. As Martha observed in her neighbors, heart trouble and longevity tend to run in families as do a host of other characteristics, infirmities, and diseases, yet not every individual in a family has the same heredity; law and chance interact. If a person develops cancer, it is not because God has decided that this person should suffer. Suffering caused by nature is generally not sent by God to punish or instruct specific victims, but is usually distributed by a combination of chance and laws of nature.

But what about Jesus' healings? Aren't these examples of God intervening in nature? Jesus' resurrection is the prime example of God's power to burst the boundaries of the present order of nature, while Jesus' healings are additional signs that God has something better in mind for the future. Yet in an overwhelming percentage of cases, God honors the existing mechanisms of nature and does not intervene to bring special punishment or special benefit. Jesus himself refused to see a man's blindness or the toppling of a tower on eighteen people as divine punishment for sin (John 9:1-3; Luke 13:4). And while Jesus' healings of certain individuals are hopeful signs of a renewed future creation without disease and infirmity, Jesus did not heal all the sick in Israel or abolish illness and disability from the world.

A third idea is that God can use suffering for good. Although God does not send specific suffering to a person, God maintains a world in which suffering occurs in order to fashion Christlike persons as citizens for God's kingdom.

We must keep our eyes on God's chief purpose for us—as individuals we are to become like Jesus Christ, and as a human community we are to become the kingdom of God. God's main purpose for us as individuals is not to be the smartest or the richest person around, but to become like Jesus Christ—to trust and obey God completely and to love others as we love ourselves. Although all the details of our lives are not divinely arranged, God is always present in the midst of those details, seeking to lead us toward greater likeness to Christ. If we find success in our endeavors, God tries to draw us toward gratitude and generosity. If we encounter obstacles or tragedy, God seeks to lead us toward greater courage, patience, and faith. God does not prearrange the suffering each of us will get, but when suffering comes, God works to help us face it with faith and good character (Rom. 8:28).

Throughout a lifetime we have a number of responsibilities and relationships, perhaps also a number of jobs, yet we have only one fundamental career—to be a son or daughter of God by trusting in God's mercy and by caring for one another. In this career, faith and love do not march effortlessly from one triumph to another; rather they face continual opposition and struggle. As Jesus learned trust, obedience, and love through trial, persecution, and pain, so we should not expect to be free of suffering; disciples are not above their master. In our prayers, then, no matter what our outward circumstances, we may cling to the words of the old spiritual: "Lord, I want to be like Jesus."

Our purpose as individuals fits with God's intention for us as a human community—to become the kingdom of God. In that kingdom people are at harmony with God, one another, and nature. In the kingdom of God, all forms of evil have been vanquished by the power of God; the fundamental sin of idolatry has been rooted out of the human heart, injustice and unkindness have been cast out of human relations, disease and death have been removed from nature. Jesus' ministry with its creation of a community of faith, its acceptance of social outcasts, and its healings was a foretaste of life in God's kingdom, just as contemporary manifestations of faith and justice are anticipations of it.

But why does God wait to bring in the kingdom in its fullness? If God is going to destroy evil in the end, why not do it now? Why maintain a natural realm in which earthquakes, floods, disease, and death plague human life? Why indeed allow humans to continue playing a part in this by misusing their freedom to bring about death and disease? There is much that we do not know. But in the meantime we know that suffering has the potential of building up human character into the likeness of Christ. The fact that life in this world depends on physical necessities makes it a place in which responsibility, trust, and caring can be molded. If a community were to pollute its water supply and God were to step in to clean it up before anyone drank it, that community would never learn to be responsible with the necessities of life and to take care of one another. If God intervened to ward off death and all other hazards in nature before they could strike us, we would remain little children who would never have our faith in God and concern for others tested by adversity. God's waiting to finally vanquish all evil and suffering, therefore, seems to be based on God's desire to have us engage in the difficult undertaking of becoming like Christ and fashioning a community of harmony. In short, if the world were a dreamland paradise in which every need were satisfied without effort or planning and no harm could come to us, it would not foster human responsibility, trust in God, or caring for one another.

These three insights on suffering caused by people and by nature give us some idea of why God would allow suffering, but they may not satisfy us on all counts. With Martha we might protest that the price Mikey and the whole family paid was too high. Why do some cancer patients endure a terrible, dragged out death? Couldn't nature have been designed in such a way that excessive suffering would be impossible? Why does some humanly caused suffering such as the killing of millions of people in World War II death camps have such awful proportions? Couldn't limits be set by God? We are unable to answer these questions, yet we are not totally in the dark. While God is not responsible for the suffering caused by human freedom and does not ordinarily send suffering caused by nature, God can use suffering to help us become more like Christ.

God's Conquest of Suffering

Why pray if God only suffers with us and over us? Family, friends, and counselors share our suffering, but we don't pray to them. The very act of praying assumes that the one to whom we pray is greater than any human being. Granted, part of God's greatness is the unique ability to share our situations fully from the inside, but doesn't that greatness also include the power to overcome suffering?

Doesn't Scripture itself say more? If the last word is that God shares the depth of our suffering, then it seems that Jesus never got beyond the cross. What about Easter and the promise of new life through resurrection? Christ's resurrection means that God not only enters into the depths of suffering, but also intends to conquer death and all the other sources of suffering; faith in the risen Christ impels us to hope for limited victories over evil even now in this life and for ultimate victory and release from the conditions that produce suffering.

People often think of resurrection as being made alive again after death, with no other major changes taking place. But in truth Christ's resurrection authorizes us to hope for a radical transformation of human life and the entire world.

Death is a basic part of the present system of things. Not only do people die, so do all living things on earth. What would it be like if nothing on earth ever died? What if every human being who had ever lived were still alive? Already we are feeling the pressures of population growth; it would be much worse if no one ever died. Imagine also what it would be like if every fly that had ever lived were still alive; we could hardly take a breath without inhaling a fly. I am not praising the benefits of death. Death, however, is so much a part of this world system, that it could not be abolished without changing the whole system.

By raising Jesus from the dead, God announced his intention to transform the world as we know it. In 1 Corinthians 15 Paul says that the risen body is a "spiritual body," as different from our present physical body as a wheat plant is from its seed. But Paul cannot describe the spiritual body. All we can really say is that it is a very different body than we are accustomed to. This is suggested also in some Gospel accounts of the risen Christ suddenly appearing to disciples gathered in a room with the doors shut; a body that can do that must be very different from our own. The resurrection of Christ is not like replacing a faulty alternator on a car with an unbroken version of the same part and leaving the rest of the car as it was; it is like creating an entirely new electrical system that is meant to fit into a dramatically new vehicle. The resurrection of Christ is a sign that God does not plan to tinker around, making a few adjustments in the present system. God intends to create a radically new world with radically new people—a new heaven and a new earth in which death, mourning, crying, and pain will be no more (Rev. 21:1-4).

This is not surprising when we consider that, in the life, death, and resurrection of Jesus Christ, God attacks the twin sources of suffering—nature and misuse of human freedom—and begins to create a new nature and a new humanity. In the life and death of Jesus, God has laid the foundation for a new humanity that uses its freedom to trust in the Lord and to care for one another. In Christ's resurrection God has created the material out of which a new universe and new human body will be fashioned. Thus our prayers, especially in time of suffering, are strengthened by this hope.

When we pray, we should cling to God's promise to transform all things in Christ. God gives us limited victories over evil in this life as we share in Christ's new humanity and as our community life bears some likeness to the peace and justice of the kingdom. God also wants us to participate in the renewal of the whole creation, when the very sources of suffering and sorrow will be banished. The life, death, and resurrection of Christ tell us not only that we have the comfort of God's presence in the midst of suffering, but also that we have hope for a new life and a new world. Prayer both expresses this hope and rests on it.

Comfort, Hope, and Confidence

One evening during a walk along the Upper Iowa River, I sat down on the dike and watched the water. This water would soon flow into the Mississippi River and then eventually into the Gulf of Mexico, a long journey. Life is like a journey on a river, and our ideas of God and our practice of prayer reflect our place on the river's course. When we move through a smooth stretch, our concept of God and our prayers mirror that security; but when we encounter rough waters, our ideas and prayers are often overturned and we flounder. Of course, before we get far we are told that the river is dangerous, but we don't really know in advance what it's like. Not until we see a beloved companion disappear below the surface, or are attacked by fellow travelers, or realize that the river water is polluted, or have unexpected rapids turn us upside down do we truly begin to recognize the perils of the journey. Unable to handle the dangers, we cry out to God to save us; we even hear others who seldom speak to God call out for God's help. If we get through the rough spot unscathed, we are grateful. But frequently the turbulence continues and even gets worse, and we get angry and frustrated with God. We want to know what sort of God would let this happen. Can we pray to such a God?

The answer is yes. In spite of our questions about suffering, we can know a comfort, a hope, and a confidence—all founded on God.

We can take comfort because God is with us throughout the journey; if the waters are rough, God shares them with us. The God who went all the way to the cross stays with us for the entire journey. This is a God to whom we can pray, for this God comforts us and heals our wounds.

We can have hope because some day God will make the river safe. The God who raised Jesus from the dead will one day transform the whole course by purifying the waters and removing the hazards. This is a God to whom we can pray, for this God of hope will ultimately deliver us from our plight.

We can have confidence as well. We are confident that God, who is with us on this dangerous journey, knows it can be for our good, for the responsibilities and challenges of the journey offer us endless opportunities for becoming more like Jesus Christ and creating in human community glimpses of the kingdom of God. This indeed is a God to whom we can pray, because this God of purpose gives us confidence that the journey is meaningful.

6

I Ask
but Nothing
Happens

LL OF US HAVE HAD THE EXPERIENCE OF ASKING God for something over and over again, yet nothing happens. At times we have been selfish in our requests, and we can understand why God wouldn't grant them. It bothers us, though, when we ask for something good, something we think God would want to give, and then it's denied or left suspended without a clear answer. It makes us question the value of coming to God with our needs and the needs of others. Since this is such an important issue, I made it the central topic of a two-day workshop with a small group of church people.

I began the workshop with some remarks about prayer as a dialog in which we speak and listen to God, and then I pointed out that one of the most frustrating things in prayer is when we ask God for something and we don't seem to get an answer. We begin to wonder whether prayer is a monologue rather than a dialog, because God doesn't appear to pay any attention. I then invited the twelve participants to contribute cases of "unanswered" prayer that we could discuss and analyze. They were cautious at first, but after a few minutes of talking around the issue one pastor presented the case of a man in a former parish whom we agreed to call Peter.

Peter was a victim of a plant closing. There had been talk of closing for quite a while, and the corporation had announced it six months in advance, but Peter couldn't afford to look seriously for another job until shortly before the end; his wages were good, and he couldn't pass up the severance pay given to those who stayed until the last. When he finally began to search for a new job, there was nothing for him. The area in which he lived was economically depressed at that time, and his age and training were against him. No one wanted a 51-year-old man whose whole work life had been spent making heavy equipment; people like him were a dime a dozen. At first, being out of work wasn't so bad emotionally and financially, but as the months wore on and the unemployment and severance money ran out, the finances got tighter and tighter. His wife's income kept them afloat. The worst part was that he felt so useless. He had worked all his adult life without realizing how much work had meant to his sense of worth. Of course, there were part-time jobs available at fast-food restaurants for minimum wage, but that would hurt his pride even more.

Throughout this whole experience Peter and his wife prayed that he would find a decent job. He didn't expect the sky; he knew it would be almost impossible to find a job with pay and benefits like what he'd had, but he hoped for something moderately good. At first he had taken heart from that petition in the Lord's Prayer, "Give us this day our daily bread." He knew they wouldn't literally starve as long as his wife had her job, but there were many things he could no longer provide for his family. What hurt most of all was that he couldn't help his second daughter with her college expenses. He had helped her older sister, but there simply was nothing to give her. So Peter persisted in asking God for a job. He read his Bible and found several passages that encouraged confidence in asking. The passage that stood out for him was Matthew 7:7-8: "Ask and it will be given to you; seek and you will find; knock and the door will be opened to you. For everyone who asks receives; he who seeks finds; and to him who knocks, the door will be opened."

Here Jesus seemed to assure Peter that he would receive whatever he asked from God. Day after day, month after month, he asked, but no job came. Peter became bitter and angry, not only with the company and the politicians, but also with God. What troubled Peter the most was the lack of any response from God. If he could be sure the answer was no, then maybe he could deal with that fact much like a person could deal with a serious disability. But he lived each day between hope and despair, and the absence of an answer from God fueled both—he hoped that maybe tomorrow God would bring him a job, he despaired because praying seemed useless. Peter kept on asking God for a job, but his heart wasn't in it anymore. He felt that God had let him down and reneged on a promise. Peter had talked with his pastor about this, but the pastor had been unable to help.

Seek First the Kingdom

After some discussion of Peter's case, our group decided the best way to deal with the issues at stake was to focus our attention on the Bible passage that had given Peter so much trouble—"Ask and it will be given to you . . ." (Matt. 7:7-8). When we interpreted these words within their context in the Sermon on the Mount (Matt. 5–7), we found they challenged us to revise our understanding of petitionary and intercessory prayer.

The theme that pervades the Sermon on the Mount is the kingdom of God and its righteousness, a righteousness that exceeds that of the scribes and Pharisees (Matt. 5:20). In the righteousness of the scribes and Pharisees, it is wrong to kill and commit adultery, but in the higher righteousness of God's kingdom it is wrong to be angry with one's brother or to look at a woman lustfully. In Matthew's understanding of the kingdom, people are children of their heavenly Father and are to treat one another as fellow children of God. The result is genuine harmony and peace. In other words, in the kingdom of God, people lead Christlike lives, for they trust and obey God and take care of one another. According to Jesus, the kingdom of God and its righteousness should have primary importance in our lives, even above concern for the basics of existence—food, drink, and clothing. "But seek first his kingdom and his righteousness, and all these things will be given to you as well" (6:33).

Therefore Jesus' assurance that "everyone who asks receives; he who seeks finds; and to him who knocks, the door will be opened" is not a promise about just any request. Jesus' words on prayer have a double thrust. First, Jesus commands us to ask, seek, and knock regarding the kingdom of God and its righteousness. In other words, Jesus tells us what to pray for above all else. Second, Jesus assures us that when we ask, seek, and knock about the kingdom, we will receive, find, and be opened unto.

Our group discussed how many of our prayers of petition and intercession would change if we followed Jesus' counsel. I said that my prayers for my own family would take on a different edge. Not only would I thank God for my parents and ask that their health be sound, but I would also ask God to strengthen them in faith, love, and hope. Besides gratefully acknowledging my wife's steadfast companionship and help, I would ask for her growth in the Christlike life. For each of my children as well I would pray first of all for their life in God and their love for others.

Our discussion group agreed that Peter was not mistaken in asking God for a job, but he was misguided in making that his primary and indeed almost his only request; he was treating the job as though his whole identity and well-being depended on it. That is idolatry. It is right to look for a job to provide the things we need and to engage in meaningful work, yet this must be done in such a way that we do not place our ultimate confidence in something other than God.

If prayer is truly dialog, then Peter's prayer had not gone unanswered, for God's silence was a response to Peter's request, just as silence can be a meaningful answer in human conversations. Unfortunately, it is often difficult to know what God's silence means, for it can mean "no" or "wait" or "think again." In any case, an extended silence should lead us to reexamine our requests. If Peter had done this, he might have come to see that his identity was not ultimately based on a job, and he would have modified his request. If Peter had listened to the silence, he might have been led to seek the kingdom of God first.

While I was saying this, a lively woman with some touches of gray in her hair was nodding her head, so I asked her if she had anything to add. Doris proceeded to tell us about her prayers during her husband's three-year bout with cancer that led to his death. It had been an awful shock when it was diagnosed, but he resolved to fight it, and except for occasional low moments, his attitude was positive and hopeful. Besides seeing doctors and taking chemotherapy, they both prayed for healing. Their priest gave him the anointing of the sick, and they knew that many members of their parish as well as relatives were praying for healing. After the first series of chemotherapy treatments, the cancer shrank and stabilized for about a year; but then it started to grow and spread. He gradually declined.

During this time, Doris found that her prayers and the prayers of her husband changed. She said that from the beginning they had asked for faith as well as healing, but their understanding of what faith meant grew over time. At first they thought that faith was mostly the confidence that God would heal. But as time went on they came to see that faith meant a great deal more. They were grateful that God had granted the year of remission so they could grow in their appreciation of one another and in their trust that, come what may, God loved them. As time went on, they could genuinely pray Jesus' prayer in Gethsemane, "My Father, if it is possible, may this cup be taken from me. Yet not as I will, but as you will" (Matt. 26:39).

Doris said that some people might claim that their request for healing had gone unanswered, but she and her husband had not felt that way. They believed that God had heard and given them more time, enabling them to grow in faith far beyond what they ever imagined or sought at the start. Far from being a time of unanswered prayer, those three years were the fullest in fellowship and dialog with God; through that dialog she and her husband had been led to seek first God's kingdom and his righteousness.

God Makes Things Happen

The next morning when I entered the conference room where our group met, several people were engaged in a lively conversation. A quick-witted young man in his late twenties was saying that he agreed with yesterday's conclusion that God uses the dialog of prayer to help us seek first the kingdom, but he argued that there are occasions when a request expresses strong loyalty to God's kingdom and yet it is still denied. He cited the case of his grandmother who recently confided to him that her chief prayer was that one of her sons (this man's uncle) might come to faith in God. She asked for other things for her son, but most of all she prayed for his conversion, for she saw faith as the pearl of great price. She paid special attention to Jesus' parable of the importunate widow who persisted in her appeals to a judge for vindication, for Jesus gave assurance that God would vindicate his faithful ones speedily. His grandmother had persisted in her intercession for about 50 years, and it was a great sorrow for her that her son showed no spark of faith in the Lord. She hadn't given up, but her grandson was wondering why her request had not been granted; surely she had placed the kingdom above all else.

He had hardly finished when a good-looking, stylishly dressed woman added that she had a similar question. Ever since she was a teenager she had been asking God for humility, because she knew vanity was a barrier between her and other people. She could see how Jesus accepted all kinds of people, and it bothered her to admit that she shied away from people unlike herself both at work and at her church. She longed to be oblivious to social distinctions. She was sure humility was a central quality of those in the kingdom of God, for Jesus had said, "Blessed are the meek," and Paul told the Christians in Rome not to think of themselves more highly than they ought. Our workshop was being held at a monastery, and the previous evening one of the monks told this woman that humility is a key virtue for Christians. So when she was asking for humility, was she not seeking first the righteousness of the kingdom of God?

Yet after praying for a number of years (she didn't specify how many), she still had a difficult struggle with vanity and pride.

The group's agenda for the morning had been very nicely provided, so I proposed to focus the rest of our discussion on these two cases. They raised the important question of whether God can be counted on to accomplish anything even when we seek the kingdom and its righteousness. We turned to the case of the grandmother who prayed for her son's conversion to faith in God.

There were questions about what was meant by "conversion" and "faith in God." Was the grandmother looking for some striking conversion experience? Was she equating faith in God with attendance at church? "No," the young man said. His uncle was a decent man but by no means a secular saint serving the needy; he had described himself at times as an atheist and at other times as a skeptic. When his son was little, he allowed his wife to take the child to Sunday school, but he made no secret of the fact that he felt religion and belief in God were just poppycock. The grandmother was simply asking God to bring her son to a basic belief and trust in God, not necessarily to make him a leading member of the church council. She was clearly putting the kingdom of God first. She asked her heavenly Father for the best of all good things; why had she not received it?

Are there limits to what God can do when we intercede for other people? Perhaps God has accepted self-imposed limits in choosing to create creatures who have some measure of freedom. This is not a restriction forced upon God; nonetheless, it is a limit that God does not wish to violate. To be sure, human freedom is more than being able to choose between breakfast cereals, for the highest freedom comes with faith and is itself a gift of the Holy Spirit; however, God allows humans the power to refuse the gift of faith. The life of faith, like prayer, is a dialog with ongoing responses back and forth; God takes the initiative and we respond, then God answers our response, and so on. Indeed, we could well say the life of faith *is* prayer, listening and responding to the God who is present within us and around us. The dialog of faith is not an interrogation, it requires our willing participation. In short, the grandmother's request that her son come to faith is one that God could not fulfill as long as the son was closed to the dialog of faith.

Another person in our group suggested that this idea had implications for prayers for peace and social justice, which are fundamental features of God's kingdom. Where there is social injustice, many have been praying decade after decade for justice. In situations of oppression, open warfare, and the threat of nuclear holocaust, countless petitions for peace have been uttered. But God will not impose social justice and peace upon us or drop them into our laps; the fact that God lets world history continue may mean that since justice and peace involve relations of human beings with one another, God wants us to participate in bringing them about.

The woman who had prayed for humility objected that this limitation did not apply in her case because she was open to God, so we focused on her repeated petitions for humility. Unlike the case of intercessory prayer, the woman was seeking a change in herself rather than in someone else. So in this situation it appeared that there was no human blockage to God's granting of her request for humility.

The case had the group stumped. They knew firsthand what she was talking about, for nearly all admitted to asking God for deliverance from some negative quality that stood in the way of more effective service to God and others—a quick temper, sexual lust, envy, and so forth. Yet most confessed that their problem had not been completely overcome; several had made gains, but none claimed to be free from struggle. They knew the reality of this experience, but now when they reflected on it, they couldn't understand why "Ask and it will be given to you" should not be fulfilled in this situation.

We humans are complex creatures, and conscious intentions make up only a fraction of our being. I know full well that on occasion I have vowed to be kind to someone who has annoyed me, and I have sincerely meant it; I genuinely wanted to forget the past and not let the person's ways bother me. I also know, however, that frequently the planting of my best intentions can not produce a flower that lasts more than a short while. The fact is that I am much more than my intentions. I am also made up of attitudes, emotions, habits, unconscious insecurities, and more. In other words, there are far more hindrances within me to God's will than I realize.

But the question remains: Why doesn't God simply deliver us from these demons once and for all when we ask for it? It's understandable that God would not free those who are in opposition, but when we honestly seek deliverance, why doesn't God give it? Isn't that what God is—a savior?

Seeking the kingdom is a long, hazardous passage similar to that taken by many who fled from the conflicts in Southeast Asia. These refugees traveled to safety and freedom on fragile boats through dangerous waters or by foot on enemy-patrolled trails. They were not suddenly lifted out of the conflict by helicopter; their escape itself was a journey filled with struggle. In like manner, God's way of being Savior usually is not to airlift us out of trials, but to guide, strengthen, and equip us for the journey of struggle against evil, while assuring us that we will eventually reach sanctuary. Of course, the journey is not all struggle and hardship, for there are many times of satisfaction, joy, pleasure, and companionship on the way. Yet real hazards, some obvious, others beguiling, are present along the way.

Jesus told us in advance that discipleship would be difficult. "If anyone would come after me, he must deny himself and take up his cross and follow me" (Matt. 16:24). As Matthew relates the story, Jesus had begun to tell his disciples that he must suffer and die, and Peter protested that this would not happen to Jesus. Jesus replied that not only must he suffer, but so must those who follow him. Just as the way of the cross for Jesus ran through his whole life of service to God and others and not just his last few hours, so also for us it spans our journeys of faith, not just certain periods of great suffering. Jesus' way of the cross was a protracted contest against sin and evil, for from the start he faced temptation, opposition, and rejection. For us to follow Jesus means a lifelong struggle against evil forces within ourselves and within our world.

Without prayer we could never make it. We simply are not wise enough or strong enough; without God's guidance through prayer we are lost. But prayer is more than just saying the same petitions over and over again as though God were hard of hearing; it is also listening for God's answer and perhaps modifying our requests accordingly. If we pray for deliverance from vanity and are not speedily granted humility, then we should realize that God is not going to helicopter us out of our difficulty but wants us to slog through. It is a mistake to conclude that God has not heard us or that God has done nothing. If we have eyes that see and ears that hear, we can discover that God makes a great deal happen.

The very fact that we have made a petition is a sign that God has been at work. When we express our wishes and feelings in prayer, we are not informing God of something new; God knows our thoughts before we utter them. But giving expression to them affects our relationship with God. On a different level this is true in human relationships as well. It is one thing to resent a fellow worker; it is quite another thing to voice that resentment. To openly express my resentment to that person has an effect on our relationship, because it gives the other person the opportunity to respond. Dialog is now possible, and maybe the relationship can be improved. However, no gain can be made if I refuse to voice my resentment. Similarly, coming to God with a request is a significant step, for we do this because the Spirit has already been at work convincing us that God is approachable.

When thinking about what God is doing to make things happen in response to prayer, we need to keep in mind God's goal for us—we are to be made like Christ and fitted for God's kingdom. That someone sees the evil of vanity and asks for humility, or discerns another's lack of faith as a great need and intercedes for faith, or recognizes that others suffer social injustice and prays for justice—these are already signs of the Christlike life of the kingdom. Furthermore, when the grandmother persists in her petition for her son's turn to faith in God, God has been conforming the grandmother to the patient compassion of Christ. Although God did not bring the woman battling vanity to perfect humility, through her moral struggles God was building her endurance and character on the journey. God was also making things happen with Doris and her dying husband; even though their petitions for healing were not finally granted, their growth in faith was in keeping with God's basic goal for us.

"Ask and it will be given to you; seek and you will find; knock and the door will be opened to you." Jesus' words are not empty. God does make things happen through prayer. It may not be what we ask for or expect, and it may not even be all that God would like to achieve, but whenever we bring our needs to God and listen for the response, God accomplishes things.

Extending Our Horizon

Although much of God's activity within ourselves, others, and the world is hidden from us, there are some basic ways of becoming more attuned to what God is doing. First, we can recall the meaning of baptism. Paul says that through baptism we have been united with Christ in a death like his and will be united with him in a resurrection like his (Rom. 6:5). While the outward forms of baptism—washing with water and saying the words of baptism—are simple actions quickly finished, the inner reality is a mystery that takes more than a lifetime to unfold. This inner reality is a union with Christ's death and resurrection that continues as we die to our old, sinful selves and live more Christlike lives. God is active in this mystery in ways often hidden from us, for only on occasion does it dawn on us how God has brought us to deeper faith and love. At the same time that God is working unseen, Paul summons us to live responsibly: "Count yourselves dead to sin but alive to God in Christ Jesus" (Rom. 6:11). To recall the meaning of baptism is therefore to remember what God is fundamentally concerned with in our lives. While each year adds new events to the chronicle of our lives, the purpose of it all is to be conformed to Jesus Christ.

A second way to become more attuned to what God is doing is to remember other believers and their experiences in prayer. For instance, the apostle Paul tells us he had a thorn in the flesh, probably a physical ailment. "Three times I pleaded with the Lord to take it away from me. But he said to me, 'My grace is sufficient for you, for my power is made perfect in weakness' " (2 Cor. 12:8-9). We cannot say for sure what Paul meant by praying for healing three times, but it apparently refers to very earnest petitioning. We do know, however, that Paul listened for an answer and received it. In this case God's answer was not to heal Paul but to give him the grace to live with his ailment. For Paul prayer was truly a dialog.

A third way to become more aware of what God is making happen is to meditate on the Lord's Prayer. The order of the petitions is significant. The one petition for our basic needs—"Give us today our daily bread"—is preceded by three petitions that deal with various aspects of the kingdom of God, "Hallowed be your name, your kingdom come, your will be done" (Matt. 6:9-10). To ask that God's name be hallowed is another way of asking for God's kingdom to come, for to the degree God's name is treated as holy, God's kingdom is present. Likewise, when God's will is done on earth as it is in heaven, God's kingly power rules. The fact that these three petitions are placed ahead of the request for daily bread is another way of seeking first the kingdom of God.

Meditating on the Lord's Prayer reminds us of God's priorities. Pondering the Lord's Prayer, rather than racing through it without much thought, is an old practice that won the approval of two sixteenth-century Christians wise in the ways of prayer. The Spanish mystic St. Teresa of Avila praised a sister nun for praying in great depth with only the Lord's Prayer. Martin Luther, when he was over 50 years old, said he still suckled at the Lord's Prayer like a child. Reflecting on the Lord's Prayer so that its petitions become our own has the effect of extending our horizons to give us a better view of what God wants to accomplish. When we pray only for the worldly success and health of ourselves and those close to us, we are praying in a valley; God's broader concerns are closed off from view. In the Lord's Prayer, Jesus teaches us to extend our horizons to the fundamentals of the kingdom of God and its righteousness at home and throughout the world.

It is a good discipline at any time, but especially when we feel God has left a request unanswered, to meditate on the Lord's Prayer. In teaching us to seek first the kingdom of God and its righteousness, the prayer expands the range of our requests. And by reminding us of God's goals for human beings, the Lord's Prayer nourishes faith that, within limits of God's own choosing, God does indeed make things happen through prayer.

7

How Important Is Prayer?

HOW IMPORTANT IS PRAYER? THIS QUESTION lies behind most of our questions and doubts about prayer. If we truly believe prayer is critical, we will have little difficulty taking time for it. If we are utterly convinced of the surpassing worth of conversation with God, we will not rely chiefly on the same old words year in and year out. And if we are sure of prayer's great value, we will not constantly be troubled by wandering thoughts during prayer. Thus the question of importance is wrapped up with most of our other questions about prayer.

When we experience and understand the reality of prayer, we come to see that prayer is of the utmost importance for the Christian life, for prayer enlivens faith in God, strengthens our bonds with others, and awakens us to the warmth of God's loving presence.

The Leaven of Faith

Jesus compared the kingdom of God to leaven or yeast "that a woman took and mixed into a large amount of flour until it worked all through the dough" (Matt. 13:33). The same image applies to faith, for, like the kingdom of God, faith is not readily observable, yet it influences the entire person. Faith, any faith, has at least three dimensions—belief, trust, and commitment—which fundamentally leaven or shape a person.

First of all, belief—holding something to be true—influences us by shaping our outlook on life. On a city street two people walk by a disheveled man who is talking out loud but not speaking to anyone in particular; he appears disoriented and is apparently homeless. One passerby thinks, "Why doesn't this bum do something constructive instead of being a nuisance?" The other thinks, "What a shame that our society lets a person sink to this level." They see the same man, but they see him differently. The reason is that they have different beliefs about the homeless.

We all hold a multitude of beliefs—beliefs about the makeup of the universe, beliefs about various groups of people, beliefs about politics, economics, religion, and so forth. All these beliefs influence our interpretation of reality, but they do not have equal weight. We can change many beliefs without relinquishing the faith that guides our lives, but some beliefs are essential to a given faith. For instance, belief in God is essential to Christian faith; without it Christian faith cannot exist. Another belief essential to Christian faith is the conviction that Jesus of Nazareth is the key to understanding who God is and what it means to be truly human. When we take this belief seriously, one result is that mercy and compassion have a large place in our outlook. Not only do we see God as forgiving, but we tend to look upon other people with compassion. Rather than thinking we are superior to those who fail or have misfortune, we feel acceptance and a common bond. The belief that mercy and compassion are qualities of God and of the truly human tends to yield a merciful and compassionate outlook on life.

Our perspective influences how we behave as citizens in the political arena of a democratic society. Whereas the general human inclination is to operate politically according to self-interest, a compassionate outlook will lead us to work and vote on behalf of needy people such as the homeless. While many see them as lazy ne'er-do-wells and act accordingly in the political arena, the compassionate person has concern for people with needs regardless of where the blame for their condition lies. Both see homeless people, but they see them differently.

Our outlook also has an impact on relationships in the family. People of all perspectives may marry and have children, but the nature of their perspective strongly affects how they treat the members of their families. While a grudge-filled person will remember an unkind word and will seek to retaliate, the person with a forgiving outlook usually forgives the wrong. The grudge-bearer sees an enemy with whom the score must be evened; the forgiving person sees a fellow sinner. Our beliefs shape us by influencing our way of seeing persons and events.

The second dimension of faith that leavens a person's life is trust. We trust many people and things every day: we trust a flight crew to take us safely to our destination; we trust the postal service to deliver our mail; we trust the chairs in which we sit to hold us up. We could not exist without trust. However, the trust that forms a person's faith is ultimate trust—what we rely on above all else. We don't place our highest trust in a flight

crew, the postal service, or a chair. The question of ultimate trust asks, On what do I depend for my basic
security?

It might seem that ultimate trust comes into play
only at those rare moments such as when a person faces
death, but that is far from the case. If our fundamental
trust is in power, for instance, our whole existence is
organized around acquiring and protecting it. Sometimes subtly, sometimes obviously, power shapes our
choices and actions. It may not determine the particular
decisions we make at work on a given day, but overall
we may treat work as a means to obtaining the security
that power seems to bring. And since power can be lost,
we may be driven by anxiety to secure it and increase
it. What we trust in above all else establishes a basic
motivation in our lives.

Commitment is the third dimension of faith that
leavens a person. While trust is the receptive, more pas-
sive side of faith, commitment is the outgoing, giving-
of-self side. Commitment is another term for love or
caring about something, for we give ourselves only to
what we care about. Again, everyone has a multitude
of commitments—personal, legal, financial, but the
deepest faith—often called religious faith—has to do
with our highest commitment. What is it that I love most
of all? This may not be easy to determine, but a good
way to discover it is to ask what the real meaning of my
life is. If I were to lose my job, and my life would still
have meaning, then my job is not my most basic commitment. But if my life would be fundamentally mean-
ingless without my wife, then she would be my ultimate
commitment.

Just as belief and trust shape the everyday stuff of
life as well as all its most memorable events, so does
commitment. A dean of Harvard University once wrote
that, when new at the position, he eagerly looked forward to a private meeting with a member of the faculty

who was a world-famous scientist. The dean asked the scientist what was the driving force behind his remarkable accomplishments. The dean felt very let down when, instead of citing lofty goals such as truth or human well-being, the scientist replied, "Fame and wealth." These were what the scientist really cared about, and they motivated his research.

Our ultimate commitment does not determine all the specific choices and actions of our lives, but it does establish the basic purpose for them. It's conceivable that another scientist could independently have made the same discoveries as the Harvard scientist and done so for a humanitarian purpose. It's also conceivable that two people could perform the same tasks at work, play on the same softball team, belong to the same social club, and attend the same church, yet do all these things with different goals in mind. It makes an enormous difference whether people see their work as just a means to earn the money to live or as one way of serving God by serving the needs of others. It matters a great deal whether a person plays on a softball team in order to gain recognition or to enjoy the God-given gifts of athletic activity and companionship with teammates and opponents alike. Our ultimate commitment is so significant because it affects the spirit with which we do the common things in the middle ground of life as well as the important and unimportant things on the edges.

Ultimate commitment also affects us by establishing our highest priority. We distribute our resources of time, energy, and money according to the level of caring and concern. Things for which we care little receive little of our attention, whereas those things about which we care very much receive most of our personal resources. Our faith determines what will be our highest priority, for the object of faith is what we care about above all else. The Harvard scientist would allocate the time and attention he'd give to family, friends, work, leisure, and communities depending on how they served (or at least did not detract from) his top priorities of fame and wealth. Thus the commitment dimension of faith has a decisive impact on how we live.

When we understand the nature of faith, it is clear that faith is indeed the yeast that leavens the whole loaf. Beliefs essential to our faith fundamentally affect how we interpret people, events, indeed all of reality. Basic trust establishes our ground of security in life. Ultimate commitment decides our basic purpose in life and determines what is of highest priority. Because our faith is the yeast that shapes us as persons, it is of highest importance in our lives, wherever we are and whatever we are doing.

Prayer Keeps Faith Alive

Two friends of mine once took a family vacation near Estes Park, Colorado. They drove into their campground just as daylight was waning, so they set up their camper, ate a late meal, and went to sleep. One of the attractions that had drawn them to this area was its great hiking trails. Since my friends were enthusiastic hikers, right after breakfast the entire family set out on one of the less-traveled trails. After being cooped up in the car all the previous day, their 14-year-old son was eager for some exercise; he set the pace. Their two younger kids followed, and the parents, keeping everyone within sight, brought up the rear. They were all experienced hikers whose muscles had been trained for long walks. Before long, though, the two parents noticed that their legs were tiring, and they were finding it difficult to keep up. Breathing hard, they increased their effort yet soon found that they were getting light-headed and had to stop. At first they were puzzled by their unaccustomed weakness, but after a few moments they realized they were feeling the affects of the high mountain altitude. Unable to take in enough oxygen from the thinner air, they were left panting, dizzy, and tired.

Without prayer, Christian faith becomes tired, weak, and eventually dies, for prayer is the breathing of faith. The dialog of prayer, listening and speaking to God, is faith breathing—inhaling and exhaling.

The listening dimension of prayer is like inhaling oxygen; it's how we take in the Word of God, whether that comes in the form of written or spoken words, the sacraments, or the lives of other Christians. It's true that prayer's inhaling, like a turtle's, often occurs in spread-out gulps that keep one going for a while, yet those gulps are absolutely essential. Just as the body's engine sputters and dies without oxygen, faith's vision dims, its vigor declines, and its life is finally extinguished unless it inhales the fresh air of God's Word with reminders of God's power and love as known in Jesus Christ.

Christian faith exhales through its speech and action. While in common usage we think of prayer as words addressed to God, we may also say that all our speech and action—insofar as they are animated by faith in God—are prayer. Just as Paul speaks of the consecrated life as the Christian's "spiritual act of worship" (Rom. 12:1), so we may speak of all faith's expressions in word and deed as prayer. If we take the more restricted meaning of prayer as speaking to God, prayer is indeed generally concentrated in a few minutes at the edges of the day. Nevertheless, these moments of speaking (and listening) are essential for powering faith's action, for they are the lifeline that connects us to the source of all energy.

Christian faith must both inhale and exhale. We Christians very commonly behave like my friends in the Colorado mountains who found themselves short of breath and weak, for we are not taking in enough oxygen. If we do not take enough time for listening to the

Word of God, faith becomes too weak to express itself in appropriate words and actions. Inhaling makes exhaling possible. Yet it's also true that we cannot just inhale and hold our breath; the rhythm of faith requires an outward movement. Christian faith breathes through the dialog of prayer, inhaling by listening and exhaling by speaking to God and by serving others in word and deed.

Strengthened and Supported

As human beings we need more than air, food, and water to live and grow; we also need the support of others. This is true of Christian faith as well. We need other Christian believers to teach, comfort, and challenge us in the faith. We would never come to faith without the witness of others (even a person reading the Bible alone has the witness of the early Christians), and it's impossible to continue in the faith without support from fellow believers.

One of the most powerful ways that Christians support one another is through prayer—praying with and for one another. Not long ago a friend called to say that she was soon having a breast removed because of a malignancy. My wife and I assured her of our prayers, and we were joined by many others. She went through the operation knowing she was supported by prayers from all across the country.

In the congregation of which I am a member, it happens time and again that a person in difficulty expresses thanks not only for cards, flowers, and visits, but also for prayers. Prayer with and for one another affirms the fundamental bond among Christians. It's not ultimately bonds of personality, culture, social class, or region that link people together in the church, for these divide more often than they unite. Faith in Jesus Christ bridges these distinctions. Prayer with and for one another strengthens human bonds by resting them on the bedrock of Christ.

The Practice of Prayer

Yes, faith is the leaven that shapes a person's life. And, yes, prayer keeps Christian faith alive. Yet the hard reality is that Christian faith does not exert its influence evenly throughout our lives, for contrary loyalties block its path. Trust in the Lord is constantly challenged by trust in self apart from God, and commitment to God competes with commitments to the gods of this world. As a result, prayer does not have the effortless character of normal breathing, and faith does not automatically shape the daily stuff or major events of our lives. In this situation, for faith to be strong enough to influence our life, prayer will be more like the trained breathing of a singer and even at times like the labored breathing of a long-distance runner straining for the finish line.

Prayer is not essentially a technique but dialog and communion with God. Yet there are practical suggestions for strengthening that dialog and communion so that the leaven of faith in God can more fully permeate our lives.

1. Be persistent in the effort to take time for prayer. If you have difficulty in setting aside time for prayer, you have plenty of company. This is a struggle for nearly every Christian, so don't give up. If you feel frustrated in prayer, keep on exploring new modes of prayer; different people find different forms of prayer effective and satisfying. However, the main point is to keep prayer a high priority. Without frequent prayer, our faith in God inevitably weakens and fails to leaven our daily life.

2. When starting prayer, scan the horizon of your life for needs and opportunities. Instead of falling into a prayer rut, keep your eyes open for those in need—an unhappy coworker, a grieving neighbor, a troubled teenager, a street beggar. The needs are there, but we tend to ignore them. Open eyes and an open heart bring the overlooked dwellers of our everyday world into our prayers.

3. Allow concerns hidden within your own mind to bubble up into your prayer. When we keep our burdens and stresses, fears and hurts hidden in the caves of our subconscious, we put a barrier between those needs and our faith in God; in essence we refuse to entrust them to God. As we saw earlier in this book, there are forms of meditation that help let the hidden concerns out into the ministering presence of God.

4. Above all, trust that God accomplishes good things through prayer. Sometimes we find it difficult to believe that God is doing anything through prayer. We do not always see that prayer makes an effective link between faith and life; in fact, the evidence may point to the opposite conclusion. Prayer at such times is an act of faith surrounded by darkness. Yet if we obey God's command, "Ask," and trust God's promise, "it will be given to you" (Matt. 7:7), we will discover that God does indeed accomplish good things through prayer.

Surely God accomplishes good things through the dialog of prayer. The very fact that we continue to listen to God is fundamental, for the message of God's will and love is what revives a lagging faith. Our most grievous troubles come when our sense of God's powerful love for us is dimmed, so to attend again and again to that love is the only pathway to renewal. When we appreciate the depth of that love, then thanks and praise come naturally.

God also accomplishes good things through the communion of prayer, for prayer helps us be aware of God's loving presence.

God's Loving Presence

Several years ago I was gone for five weeks on a trip to Greece, South Africa, Zimbabwe, Tanzania, and England. There had been very little communication with my family during that time. I had sent several letters and received two from my wife, and we had talked on the phone from England and again very hurriedly from New York as I informed her that I would be coming home on an earlier flight. At last my wife and I were together. Of course, we had a great deal to talk about—I bubbling over with a surplus of new experiences impossible to condense, Marion reporting on family, community, and work events over the preceding weeks. But underneath all the words, what delighted me most was her sheer presence. As we were driving home I reached over and touched her. She was not merely an image in my memory or the writer of a letter or a disembodied voice on the telephone; she was with me.

Even now Marion's presence supports and warms me. Recently our younger son went off to college, and now Marion and I are alone together. People ask us how we are coping with the empty nest syndrome, and we answer, "Just fine." We love our daughter and two sons dearly and treasure being in touch with them and their lives, yet we are finding that this time together without children at home is immensely rich and enjoyable. At the dinner table we talk, of course, about events of the day, but what we value most is simply being with one another without other persons or obligations dividing our attention. Much of the time we say very little to one another, but we frequently hug or touch hands as we pass. Naturally we have differences of opinion and times of conflict, but undergirding our entire relationship are deep loyalty and trust. Above all else, what her often quiet presence communicates to me is that I am loved, valued, and accepted.

Marion's presence accompanies me through life. When I am successful or happy, her presence invites me to share my joy with her. When I am anxious over something, her presence reassures me. Sometimes her presence reminds me that I have hurt or disappointed her, and sometimes it calls my behavior into question. Other times she is present as one who needs me. Often she is present as one with whom I share common plans and a common love for our children. Always she is present as my closest friend.

I value Marion above every other earthly good, yet I know her presence with me has definite limits. She is unable to be with me wherever I go, for we both can only be in one place at a time. Moreover, her presence with me is vulnerable to loss. Usually it does not enter into consciousness, but from time to time I realize that she could be taken from me by death or terrible disease. This awareness might be triggered by news of someone else losing a spouse or by remembrance of the fragility of life. Whatever occasions the recognition of our vulnerability, I feel as though clouds have covered the sun of her presence; for a moment I feel how cold and desolate life without her would be. Even more precious, then, is the time remaining in the warmth and light of her presence.

One of the marvels of prayer is that it brings us into awareness of God's presence. This is a presence that is not subject to the limitations of space and time; the Lord is present with us at all times and wherever we go. Neither is God's presence threatened by death and disease. Only our own blindness can close us off from that presence.

Certainly God challenges much that is lacking in our lives. And certainly God awakens feelings of awe and mystery. But most of all Jesus shows us that God loves us and seeks what is ultimately best for us. What prayer does again and again is to bring us into that loving, nurturing presence.

Sometimes when I pray I receive an image of myself sitting on one of God's knees; I'm turned part way so I can look directly into God's face, and I can feel God's arm around my shoulders giving me a gentle embrace. Some days I come knowing I've been a disappointment. Other days I'm red-faced with anger and frustration, sputtering indignant protest and demanding immediate justice. Most days I come with a rather indifferent attitude much like a child who simply takes it for granted that this is what a parent is for. When the image pops into my mind, though, the wonder of it all strikes me, and I see what a miracle it is that I am sitting on God's knee, being embraced by the Lord, and talking with the One who loves me for eternity. It's then that I also realize that I'm always sitting on God's knee when I pray, I'm always in that presence that values and accepts me. Prayer is the time when I can simply bask in that love.

How important is prayer? As important as faith in God. As important as breathing. As important as being in the presence of Love.

Questions for Reflection or Discussion

Chapter 1: I Don't Pray Enough

1. Have solitude and silence helped you when you pray? What has worked for you even when you couldn't be alone or in a quiet place?
2. Some people pray primarily in obedience to God's command to pray, while others pray in response to God's *invitation* to pray. Why might the second perspective help you feel more positive about praying?

Chapter 2: My Prayers Are Repetitious

1. What are some of the reasons for and against having children pray the same prayers each day? Are any of those reasons also valid for adults?
2. Which of the four ways of listening (reading, writing, following a daily liturgy, and taking a retreat) been meaningful to you? At what times in your life?

Chapter 3: My Mind Wanders

1. Which of the suggestions given by the author have been helpful to you when your mind wanders as you pray? Have you thought of other ideas as well?
2. Watchful prayer helped Robert see how competition was twisting his life. What might prayer reveal to you and me?

Chapter 4: I Pray Yet God Seems Distant

1. When have you had an experience of special nearness to God? How do we know God is with us even when we don't feel anything special?
2. The stories of Irene and Norman show how other people's concern and prayers support us. Have there been times when you have been either a giver or a receiver of such support?

Chapter 5: What Sort of God Would Let That Happen?

1. In the story about Martha, do you agree with her brother Roger that God arranges all the details of our lives? What role do you think human freedom plays?
2. Do you find comfort in the suggestion that since nature operates a lot by chance, some suffering can be attributed to that? Think of some examples that might apply.
3. How do the life, death, and resurrection of Jesus Christ give us hope, not just for more life, but for transformed life?

Chapter 6: I Ask but Nothing Happens

1. Have you had times when you changed your prayers as the months went by with no clear answer from God to your petitions?
2. Why doesn't God just quickly resolve our problems and negative patterns for us (vanity, temper, addictions). What positive changes happen to us as we struggle, with God's help, against them?

Chapter 7: How Important Is Prayer?

1. How has prayer helped you realize the depth of God's love for you? How important is prayer in keeping your relationship with God alive and healthy?
2. This book has shown that, even though we may experience difficulties, prayer is essential to our faith and enriches our lives. Which parts of the book spoke most clearly to you? Which of its ideas are you putting into practice?

Suggested Books

Prayer

Bloom, Anthony. *Beginning to Pray*. New York: Paulist Press, 1982.

Brandt, Leslie F. *Book of Christian Prayer*. Minneapolis: Augsburg, 1974.

Edwards, Tilden. *Living in the Presence: Disciplines for the Spiritual Heart*. San Francisco: Harper & Row, 1987.

Ensley, Eddie. *Prayer That Heals Our Emotions*. Rev. ed. San Francisco: Harper & Row, 1988.

Hammarskjöld, Dag. *Markings*. New York: Ballantine, Epiphany Books, 1985.

Kelsey, Morton T. *Adventure Inward: Christian Growth through Personal Journal Writing*. Minneapolis: Augsburg, 1980.

———. *The Other Side of Silence: A Guide to Christian Meditation*. New York: Paulist Press, 1976.

Main, John. *Present Christ*. New York: Crossroad, 1986.

Mattison, Judith. *Life Is Good, Life Is Hard: Meditations for Daily Living*. Minneapolis: Augsburg, 1987.

Merton, Thomas. *Love & Living*. Edited by Naomi Burton Stone and Patrick Hart. New York: Harcourt Brace Jovanovich, 1985.

————. *New Seeds of Contemplation*. Rev. ed. New York: New Directions, 1972.

Nouwen, Henri J. M. *Reaching Out: The Three Movements of the Spiritual Life*. Garden City: Doubleday, 1975.

————. *With Open Hands*. Notre Dame: Ave Maria, 1972.

Pennington, Basil. *Daily We Touch Him: Practical Religious Experiences*. Garden City: Doubleday, 1977.

Rogness, Alvin. *My Personal Prayer Book*. Minneapolis: Augsburg, 1988.

Simundson, Daniel J. *Where Is God in My Praying?: Biblical Responses to Eight Searching Questions*. Minneapolis: Augsburg, 1986.

Comfort in Suffering

Beker, J. Christian. *Suffering and Hope: The Biblical Vision and the Human Predicament*. Philadelphia: Fortress, 1987.

Hall, Douglas John. *God and Human Suffering: An Exercise in the Theology of the Cross*. Minneapolis: Augsburg, 1986.

Martin, James. *Suffering Man, Loving God*. San Francisco: Harper & Row, 1990.

Mitchell, Kenneth R., and Herbert Anderson. *All Our Losses, All Our Griefs: Resources for Pastoral Care*. Philadelphia: Westminster, 1983.

Schuchardt, Erika. *Why Is This Happening to Me?: Guidance and Hope for Those Who Suffer*. Translated by Karen Leube. Minneapolis: Augsburg, 1988.

Simundson, Daniel J. *Hope for All Seasons: Biblical Expressions of Confidence in the Promises of God*. Minneapolis: Augsburg, 1988.

————. *Where Is God in My Suffering?: Biblical Responses to Seven Searching Questions*. Minneapolis: Augsburg, 1983.

Wold, Stephen A. *Is God Still Here?: The Comfort of the Cross for Those Who Suffer*. Minneapolis: Augsburg, 1989.